EYE ON
Art

ANCIENT EGYPTIAN
ART AND
ARCHITECTURE

by Don Nardo

LUCENT BOOKS
A part of Gale, Cengage Learning

GALE
CENGAGE Learning™

Detroit • New York • San Francisco • New Haven, Conn • Waterville, Maine • London

LIBRARY OF CONGRESS CATALOGING-IN-PUBLICATION DATA

Nardo, Don, 1947-
  Ancient Egyptian art and architecture / by Don Nardo.
    p. cm. -- (Eye on art)
  Includes bibliographical references and index.
  ISBN 978-1-4205-0674-7 (hardcover)
  1. Art, Egyptian. 2. Art, Ancient--Egypt. 3. Architecture, Ancient--Egypt.
  4. Egypt--Antiquities. I. Title. II. Series: Eye on art.
  N5350.N37 2012
  709.32--dc22
                                                        2011020116

Lucent Books
27500 Drake Rd
Farmington Hills MI 48331

ISBN-13: 978-1-4205-0674-7
ISBN-10: 1-4205-0674-9

Printed in the United States of America
1 2 3 4 5 6 7 15 14 13 12 11

Printed by Bang Printing, Brainerd, MN, 1st Ptg., 09/2011

CONTENTS

Foreword

"Art has no other purpose than to brush aside . . . everything that veils reality from us in order to bring us face to face with reality itself."

—French philosopher Henri-Louis Bergson

Some thirty-one thousand years ago, early humans painted strikingly sophisticated images of horses, bison, rhinoceroses, bears, and other animals on the walls of a cave in southern France. The meaning of these elaborate pictures is unknown, although some experts speculate that they held ceremonial significance. Regardless of their intended purpose, the Chauvet-Pont-d'Arc cave paintings represent some of the first known expressions of the artistic impulse.

From the Paleolithic era to the present day, human beings have continued to create works of visual art. Artists have developed painting, drawing, sculpture, engraving, and many other techniques to produce visual representations of landscapes, the human form, religious and historical events, and countless other subjects. The artistic impulse also finds expression in glass, jewelry, and new forms inspired by new technology. Indeed, judging by humanity's prolific artistic output throughout history, one must conclude that the compulsion to produce art is an inherent aspect of being human, and the results are among humanity's greatest cultural achievements: masterpieces such as the architectural marvels of ancient Greece, Michelangelo's perfectly rendered statue *David*, Vincent van Gogh's visionary painting *Starry Night*, and endless other treasures.

The creative impulse serves many purposes for society. At its most basic level, art is a form of entertainment or the means

5

for a satisfying or pleasant aesthetic experience. But art's true power lies not in its potential to entertain and delight but in its ability to enlighten, to reveal the truth, and by doing so to uplift the human spirit and transform the human race.

One of the primary functions of art has been to serve religion. For most of Western history, for example, artists were paid by the church to produce works with religious themes and subjects. Art was thus a tool to help human beings transcend mundane, secular reality and achieve spiritual enlightenment. One of the best-known, and largest-scale, examples of Christian religious art is the Sistine Chapel in the Vatican in Rome. In 1508 Pope Julius II commissioned Italian Renaissance artist Michelangelo to paint the chapel's vaulted ceiling, an area of 640 square yards (535 sq. m). Michelangelo spent four years on scaffolding, his neck craned, creating a panoramic fresco of some three hundred human figures. His paintings depict Old Testament prophets and heroes, sibyls of Greek mythology, and nine scenes from the Book of Genesis, including the Creation of Adam, the Fall of Adam and Eve from the Garden of Eden, and the Flood. The ceiling of the Sistine Chapel is considered one of the greatest works of Western art and has inspired the awe of countless Christian pilgrims and other religious seekers. As eighteenth-century German poet and author Johann Wolfgang von Goethe wrote, "Until you have seen this Sistine Chapel, you can have no adequate conception of what man is capable of."

In addition to inspiring religious fervor, art can serve as a force for social change. Artists are among the visionaries of any culture. As such, they often perceive injustice and wrongdoing and confront others by reflecting what they see in their work. One classic example of art as social commentary was created in May 1937, during the brutal Spanish civil war. On May 1 Spanish artist Pablo Picasso learned of the recent attack on the small Basque village of Guernica by German airplanes allied with fascist forces led by Francisco Franco. The German pilots had used the village for target practice, a three-hour bombing that killed sixteen hundred civilians. Picasso, living in Paris, channeled his outrage over the massacre into his painting *Guernica,* a black, white, and gray mural that depicts dismembered animals and fractured human figures whose faces are contorted in agonized expressions. Initially, critics and the public condemned the painting as an incoherent hodgepodge, but the work soon came to be seen as a powerful antiwar statement and remains an iconic symbol of the violence and terror that dominated world events during the remainder of the twentieth century.

The impulse to create art—whether painting animals with crude pigments on a cave wall, sculpting a human form from marble, or commemorating human tragedy in a mural—thus serves many purposes. It offers an entertaining diversion, nourishes the imagination and the spirit, decorates and beautifies the world, and chronicles the age. But underlying all these functions is the desire to reveal that which is obscure—to illuminate, clarify, and perhaps ennoble. As Picasso himself stated, "The purpose of art is washing the dust of daily life off our souls."

The Eye on Art series is intended to assist readers in understanding the various roles of art in society. Each volume offers an in-depth exploration of a major artistic movement, medium, figure, or profession. All books in the series are beautifully illustrated with full-color photographs and diagrams. Riveting narrative, clear technical explanation, informative sidebars, fully documented quotes, a bibliography, and a thorough index all provide excellent starting points for research and discussion. With these features, the Eye on Art series is a useful introduction to the world of art—a world that can offer both insight and inspiration.

Introduction

"No Word for Art"

His hands shaking and his stomach filled with butterflies, on November 26, 1922, English archaeologist Howard Carter approached a partially buried door made of mud bricks. Whatever lay beyond that puzzling portal, he surmised, had not seen the light of day for more than thirty-two centuries. Carter had long searched for ancient royal tombs and artifacts in Egypt's Valley of the Kings. This is the modern-day name for a secluded, very dry and rugged area on the Nile River's west bank not far from the ruins of the ancient Egyptian city of Thebes.

Carter and his fellow researchers realized that some of the pharaohs, or kings, of ancient Egypt had used the valley as a necropolis, or burial ground. Afraid that their tombs would be looted by thieves, these rulers had rejected the notion of public tombs, such as pyramids, and opted instead for secret crypts in the rocky ground on which Carter now stood. In particular, he and his friend, the Earl of Carnarvon, an amateur digger, wanted to find the tomb of Tutankhamun—"King Tut" for short. At the time, extremely little was known about this pharaoh who had died young under mysterious circumstances in about 1344 B.C. (This and the other ancient Egyptian dates that follow are approximate. Historical sources vary when dating lives and events from the period.)

After years of investigation, Carter and Carnarvon (accompanied by Lady Carnarvon) stood, nearly breathless, before the door to the long-lost burial chamber. Carter himself later recalled the history-making moment:

> With trembling hands I made a tiny breach in the upper left hand corner [of the door]. Then, widening the hole a little, I inserted the candle and peered in. . . . At first I could see nothing, [but] presently, as my eyes grew accustomed to the light, details of the room emerged slowly from the mist, strange animals, statues, and gold—everywhere the glint of gold. . . . I was struck dumb with amazement, and when Lord Carnarvon [asked] anxiously, "Can you see anything?" it was all I could do to get out the words, "Yes, wonderful things!"[1]

English archeologist Howard Carter views the sarcophagus and mummy of Tutankhamun in his tomb. The tomb contained a treasure trove of ancient Egyptian art.

A Treasure Trove

What was indeed wonderful was that there were any "things" at all in the boy-king's tomb. Numerous ancient Egyptian tombs had been uncovered prior to Carter's discovery. However, they were empty because their contents had been stolen by grave robbers, mostly in ancient times. In contrast, in a fantastic stroke of good fortune, Tut's tomb was nearly intact, and there, before the eyes of the stunned excavators, lay more than two thousand beautifully preserved ancient objects.

One of these items, the astounded Carter found, was Tut's mummified body, resting inside a magnificent coffin made of three hundred pounds of solid gold. A mere fraction of the other artifacts in the burial vault included a kingly throne decorated with gold and precious gems; expertly carved figurines and statues; gorgeous jewelry items and intricately embellished perfume boxes; full-sized boats and chariots, also superbly decorated; cedarwood chests, one bearing splendid carvings of the ankh, the Egyptian symbol of life; many handsome weapons, including small swords with elaborately carved handles; an elegant gaming board with hand-carved ivory pieces; and the list goes on and on. All of the items in the tomb had been placed there for the deceased pharaoh's use in the afterlife.

In spite of their wide range of designs and uses, these many and diverse grave goods had something in common. Namely, they were all the work of talented artisans—craftsmen and artists who make things by hand. In fact, Tut's tomb was a veritable treasure trove of ancient Egyptian arts and crafts.

All ancient peoples possessed distinct forms of artistic expression and produced items that can be categorized as art. But the Egyptians, more than some others, were particularly concerned with the aesthetic (visual and artistic) qualities of the objects they fashioned, including many everyday objects. As a result, their culture turned out an enormous quantity of artwork. These include architecture, sculpture, painting, and all manner of fine craftwork. The latter included beautifully made stone vessels; exquisite jewelry made of gold, silver, and multicolored gems; high-quality, hand-carved wooden furniture items; and stunning glass objects. Surviving examples of most of Egypt's arts show clearly that the artists and artisans who created them were every bit as inventive and skilled as their counterparts in other ancient cultures. In fact, noted scholar Lionel Casson wrote before his death in 2009:

> The architects, sculptors, painters, [and others,] who created the art of ancient Egypt bear comparison with those of any age. Their achievements not only reached aesthetic heights, but they represent technological marvels as well, for the Egyptians executed their masterpieces with the most rudimentary of tools. The remarkable record of their artistic excellence can be read in works as majestic as their great temples and as delicate as their intricate jeweled clasps.[2]

Moreover, the styles and excellence of these endeavors significantly influenced the arts of neighboring peoples in both ancient and later times. As Casson put it:

> From prehistoric days, craftsmen of the Nile had displayed a sense of beauty and symmetry that touched even the most utilitarian [practical] objects—flint knives, stone or pottery household vessels, pins and combs of bone or shell. With the advent of the pharaohs, this aesthetic quality flowered into a mature art, distinctively Egyptian in concept and character. For the next 3,000 years, Egypt produced a graceful and spirited art, which served, among other things, to inspire the great Greek sculptors and artists who followed them centuries later.[3]

Artisans Who Remain Anonymous

Considering the high quality of most ancient Egyptian art, it may seem logical to assume that the artists and craftsmen who created it were widely respected and very well paid. However, that assumption is based on modern standards that did not apply in many ancient cultures. The surprising fact is that most Egyptian artisans were members of the lower classes and viewed simply as everyday workers. Indeed, with few exceptions they were treated like and paid the same as ordinary laborers who had no special training or talents.

This attitude toward artists was reflected in Egypt's overall beliefs and even its language. Egyptian culture "had no word for art and no concept of art for art's sake," scholar Rita M. Freed points out. Under such conditions, Egyptian artisans rarely signed their works or became known to anyone outside of their immediate circle of family, friends, and employers. "Despite the splendor of their works, colossal or miniature," Freed continues, "the artisans of ancient Egypt have revealed remarkably little about themselves. Most [of these] artisans remain anonymous and can only rarely be associated with a specific work."[4]

This shortage of knowledge about ancient artisans, most of whom led lower-class lives, is not unusual. In fact, archaeologists and historians have long been hindered in their work by a general lack of surviving information about ordinary folk in past ages. The vast majority of ancient historians and writers focused almost exclusively on wealthy, powerful, and high-placed individuals. Practically all of the surviving writings from Egypt and other ancient lands therefore deal with the rich and famous and pay little or no attention to the poorer folk, who made up the bulk of the population.

Furthermore, most surviving examples of ancient fine arts and crafts were owned or financed by members of the upper classes. These examples include palaces, temples, and other large buildings; durable weapons and armor; chariots; statues and busts; wall paintings; well-made furniture; expensive jewelry, dinnerware, and vases; and so forth. In contrast, people of lesser means almost never owned such things. Also, their homes and belongings were nearly always made of perishable materials that rotted away over the centuries. In most cases, therefore, after they died their names and very existence were forgotten.

In a twist of fate, however—one that is fortunate for later generations—ancient Egypt's mostly unnamed artisans left behind a kind of collective immortality. The fact remains that they actually made most of the fine arts and crafts owned and used by upper-class people. That included the numerous magnificent objects found in King Tut's last resting place. Thus, although these talented individuals remain mostly unidentified and precious little is known about their personal lives, the splendid fruits of their labors live on for people today, and in future ages as well, to marvel at and enjoy.

Monument Builders: The Crews, Tools, and Methods

On a flat, arid patch of land called Giza, near modern-day Cairo, Egypt, stand three truly majestic structures—the so-called Great Pyramids. The biggest one, erected in about 2570 B.C., covers some 13 acres (5.3ha) and was included in the prestigious list of the seven wonders of the ancient world. These and other towering pyramids, built as tombs for Egypt's pharaohs, were not the only examples of monumental, or large-scale, architecture in ancient Egypt. There were also splendid palaces, massive fortresses, and enormous temples, to name only a few.

One complex, or cluster, of temples—at Karnak, near the ancient Egyptian capital of Thebes—covers half a square mile (1.3 sq. km) and in its heyday employed more than eighty thousand priests, artisans, groundskeepers, and other personnel. Egyptologist Peter Der Manuelian of Boston's Museum of Fine Arts calls it "the most impressive Egyptian monument after the pyramids of Giza."[5] These and other similarly grand structures show that monumental architecture was the biggest and most awe-inspiring of ancient Egypt's arts.

Building by Committee

The persons who designed ancient Egypt's great temples were the ancient equivalent of modern-day architects. Today an architect comes up with the entire design for a proposed building, a detailed blueprint that skilled engineers, craftsmen, and laborers then follow to create the structure. In ancient Egypt, however, the process of designing a monumental building seems to have been more of a collaborative, or shared, effort. The pharaoh set the process in motion by calling for a structure to be built. Then a committee of men, including government administrators, scribes (persons who could read and write), and master craftsmen, met. In the words of University of Manchester scholar Rosalie David, they

> decided upon the orientations [positioning] of the monument (using astronomical observations) and determined how they would deal with any building problems. They also organized . . . the building plans and programs, and technicians who executed the work. Construction and decoration of a tomb, temple, [or other large structure,] was carried out by craftsmen who worked together under a master [expert in a specific art or task]. They included quarrymen, sculptors, painters, carpenters, and metalsmiths.[6]

One of a few notable exceptions to this procedure was the case of the renowned architect Imhotep. He was vizier (chief administrator) to the pharaoh Djoser (reigned 2667–2648 B.C.) and highly respected for his medical knowledge. Imhotep was also a gifted builder. In fact, later ancient historians credited him with the invention of stone construction. It appears that almost completely on his own, like a modern-day architect, he conceived the materials and layout for the first Egyptian pyramid-tomb and directed the construction phase as well. Called the Step Pyramid (at Saqqara, a few miles south of Giza), it is also the earliest known large stone structure. That building "incorporates many architectural innovations and new

The great complex at Karnak covered half a square mile and employed more than eighty thousand priests, artisans, groundskeepers, and construction workers.

building materials and techniques," David points out. Thereafter, most Egyptian builders "followed the traditions that" Imhotep and a few other early architects had "laid down for architectural designs."[7]

The Construction Crews

The Egyptian builders who followed Imhotep needed more than traditional designs and a group of master craftsmen to aid and advise them. They also required large crews of artisans and laborers to quarry, drag, lift, carve, and decorate the stones. Today many of these jobs are partly or fully done by machines. But the ancient Egyptians possessed no machines. All they had at their disposal were very simple tools, which meant that most of the work had to be accomplished by the muscle power of large numbers of people. Finding, organizing, and supervising these enormous crews was a major undertaking that taxed Egypt's government officials. As one modern-day expert explains,

The man who designed the Step Pyramid at Saqqara for the pharaoh Djoser went by the name Imhotep. Extremely little is known for certain about Imhotep's life and achievements beyond his work on Djoser's pyramid. Various clues uncovered by archaeologists suggest that this talented architect was also Djoser's vizier and that in addition to the Step Pyramid, he designed a temple honoring Egypt's sun god, Ra. Over time, various legends grew up about Imhotep, including one that said he was a great healer who accumulated much medical knowledge. Another legend claimed he was an almost infallible wise man. Still another said he was semidivine—the son of the creator god Ptah. Putting such legends aside, it can be said with confidence that Imhotep was the first architect in history whose name and greatest building are both preserved.

Imhotep is credited with building the first monumental structure in stone, the Step Pyramid at Saqqara, seen here in a reconstruction.

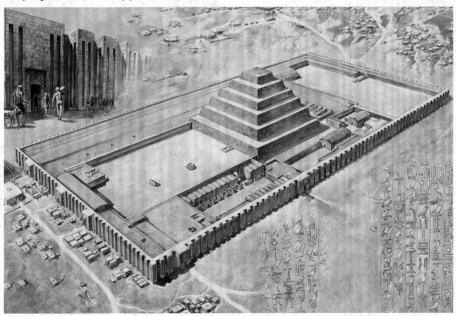

for the creation of a monstrous structure such as a pyramid, palace, or temple,

> hundreds of thousands of cubic meters of limestone and sandstone, alabaster, granite and basalt were quarried from the cliffs along the Nile Valley and the surrounding deserts. Hundreds of boatloads of timber had to be imported from [Palestine, because Egypt had no large forests, and] large quantities of tools and other equipment had to be produced. [In addition], mountains of sand and Nile mud had to be moved for the fabrication of brick. Finally, all this vast amount of material had to be brought to the construction site and lifted into position. For this purpose, thousands of people had to be conscripted [recruited] according to complicated procedures, and steered to the many building projects. These people had to be trained, fed, and clothed.[8]

It used to be thought that these workers who erected Egypt's imposing stone structures were slaves forced into service by cruel taskmasters. This was certainly the way it was depicted in most movies. Both the 1923 and 1956 versions of Cecil B. DeMille's *The Ten Commandments*, for instance, had scenes of Hebrew slaves being whipped as they toiled in the hot sun to build a new city for the pharaoh Ramesses II. Howard Hawks's *Land of the Pharaohs* (1955), a depiction of the building of King Khufu's pyramid at Giza, had similar scenes.

These and other popular films about ancient Egypt were partly inspired by fifth-century-B.C. Greek historian Herodotus's account of his visit to that land. His trip took place many centuries after the Pyramids and most other huge buildings had been raised. By that time even the most educated Egyptians could not remember how those structures had been erected. So the stories they told Herodotus were laced with guesses and pure fabrication. According to the book he wrote based on such stories, the pharaoh Khufu (whom the historian called Cheops) turned his own people into slaves and forced them "to drag blocks of stone from the quarries." The backbreaking work "went on in three monthly shifts, a hundred thousand men in a shift," and finishing the enormous pyramid "took twenty years."[9]

As it turned out, however, Herodotus and his Egyptian sources were sorely mistaken. Modern-day archaeologists and historians eventually found conclusive evidence showing that ancient Egyptian builders and construction workers were not

TOMBS OF THE PYRAMID BUILDERS

In 1990 an ancient cemetery was found on the Giza plateau, not far from the Great Pyramids. It contains many tombs of construction workers who toiled to build those huge monuments. Egypt's leading archaeologist, Zahi Hawass, later wrote:

The lower part of the cemetery contains about 600 graves for workmen and 30 larger tombs, perhaps for overseers. The tombs come in a variety of forms: stepped domes, beehives, and gabled roofs. Two to six feet high, the domes covered simple rectangular grave pits, following the configuration of the pyramids in an extremely simplified form. One small tomb featured a miniature ramp leading up and around its dome. Could the builder have intended it to represent the construction ramp of a royal pyramid? Other tombs resemble miniature mastabas with tiny courtyards and stone false doors with the names and titles of the deceased inscribed on them. . . . Inscribed in crude hieroglyphs, they record the names of the people whose skeletons lay below. On one stele [stone slab] a man named Khemenu is depicted sitting at an offering table in front of his wife, Tep-em nefret. A false door is inscribed with a woman's name, Hetep-repyt . . . [and] another belongs to Hy, priestess of the goddess Hathor, Lady of (the) Sycamore Tree, and her son Khuwy.

Zahi Hawass. "The Discovery of the Tombs of the Pyramid Builders at Giza." Guardian's Egypt. www.guardians.net/hawass/buildtomb.htm.

slaves. Instead, they were mostly farmers, shopkeepers, and craftsmen who labored on such projects on a part-time basis. The farmers sometimes worked on government projects between the planting and harvest seasons, for example, when they had some free time.

Apparently, the workers performed these labors for two reasons. First, working on government construction crews fulfilled some or all of their tax obligations. This sort of work is called corvée, or conscripted, labor. Corvée labor was so ingrained in Egyptian society that most citizens took part in it at least once in their lifetimes. Another example of the importance of such labor was uncovered by modern-day excavators. In tombs of government officials and nobles, they found many miniature figurines. These represented corvée laborers who, it was thought, would do any menial work the gods might call on the dead person to perform. Some evidence suggests that as part of the agreement between the laborers and the government, the latter supplied the former with enough food to feed their families during the construction process.

Archaeologists excavate the tombs of ancient workers near the Giza Pyramids in 2010. The tombs provide conclusive evidence that the workers were not slaves but paid artisans.

The second motivation for working on large-scale government architectural projects was a mixture of patriotic and religious duties. It was likely viewed as an honor to work directly for the pharaoh, and the laborers seem to have expected that the gods would reward them later, in the afterlife, for that work. Bearing this out are the words of an inscription found in a temple near a pyramid: "O all you gods who shall cause this pyramid and this construction of the king to be fair and [to] endure [forever], you [priests and others involved in the project] shall be effective, you shall be strong, you shall have [everlasting] souls."[10] Thus, says scholar Jill Kamil, "it was a reciprocal [mutual] service relationship [between the government and the laborers] which obviously worked. The size and splendor of the pyramids [and other large architectural works] stand as evidence."[11]

Organizing and Housing the Crews

To make the work more efficient, the crews who erected a monumental structure—the largest example of ancient Egyptian art—were organized into construction gangs. The biggest known gangs had two thousand men each. Such a unit broke down into two gangs of one thousand men, each of which was divided into five two-hundred-man groups called *zaa*. Each of the *zaa* was still further divided into groups of ten to twenty workers. Gangs of all sizes had slang names, some of which were colorful by both ancient and modern standards. The late renowned expert on Egyptian pyramids, I.E.S. Edwards, wrote that the workers often

> painted the names of their gangs . . . on the [stone] blocks before they were taken from the quarry. Although these names were very often erased in the course of subsequent operations, enough remains to perpetuate [the names of] many of the gangs. [Examples include] "Stepped Pyramid Gang," "Boat Gang," "Vigorous Gang," "Scepter Gang," "Enduring Gang," "North Gang," and "South Gang."[12]

A walled craftsmen's village is shown near the Valley of the Kings. About one hundred stonecutters and artisans lived here while building the tombs in the valley.

Having found these names painted onto stone blocks, archaeologists could identify many of the groups of artisans and laborers who erected Egypt's great monuments. But for a long time the excavators could not figure out where these people lived during the construction process. Eventually, however, several workers' villages were unearthed. One was found in the 1990s on the Giza plateau near the three Great Pyramids. The houses, which have largely disintegrated over the centuries, were mostly crude shacks made of river reeds and/or mud bricks.

Cemeteries and bakeries for the construction crews and their families were also uncovered. Describing the modest grave sites of the workers and their relatives, Egypt's leading archaeologist, Zahi Hawass, says that they come

> in a variety of forms: stepped domes, beehives, and gabled roofs. Two to six feet high, the domes covered simple rectangular grave pits. . . . We have found many false doors and stelae [stone markers] attached to these tombs. Inscribed in crude hieroglyphs, they record the names of the people whose skeletons lay below. . . .

> Study of the[se] remains . . . reveals that males and fe-
> males were equally represented, mostly buried in fetal
> positions, with face to the east and head to the north.[13]

About the bakeries, Hawass writes that each was

> about 17 feet long and eight feet wide. Inside each
> room lay a pile of broken bread pots discarded after the
> last batch of bread was removed 4,600 years ago. . . .
> Along the east wall were two lines of holes in a shallow
> trench, resembling an egg carton. The holes had held
> dough-filled pots while hot coals and ash in the trench
> baked the bread.[14]

Tools for Quarrying and Dressing

The workers who dwelled in these villages had a limited range of simple tools available to them. These included stone knives, axes, chisels, saw blades, and picks. Hammers made of wood or stone were also employed. Sharp stone edges were made by the process of knapping, or chipping. This consisted of using a hunk of extremely hard and durable stone, like dolerite or basalt, to reshape a piece of softer stone, like flint, jasper, or chert. To add an extra sharp edge to a tool, a person rubbed it vigorously with a piece of sandstone, in some ways an ancient version of today's sandpaper.

In addition to stone tools, which had originated in Egypt's dim past, metal tools were employed for some tasks. Copper knives and saws came into use in the third millennium (the 2000s) B.C., and bronze versions became common in the early second millennium B.C. Iron tools, which were harder and more durable than the copper and bronze varieties, replaced some stone construction tools in the first millennium B.C. But a number of workers still retained more traditional stone implements.

Both stone and metal tools were used to cut and shape several kinds of stone. To create their architectural wonders, Egyptian builders used both softer kinds, including limestone and sandstone, and, in lesser amounts, harder kinds like granite and basalt. Whichever type of stone was chosen for a particular project, it first had to be cut into individual blocks at the quarry. Some quarries were open, meaning the stone the builders wanted lay on the surface of the ground. The Egyptians also exploited closed quarries, which were located underground and required the digging of tunnels to reach the desired stone.

The first step in extracting the blocks from the quarry was to outline their shapes using paint or chisel marks. Then workers softened a block's surface by inducing sudden temperature changes. This was done by shoveling hot coals over the stone's surface, waiting a little while, and then pouring cold water over the heated block. With the stone suitably softened, the quarrymen held flint or dolerite chisels against its surface. They then pounded that surface with hammers, causing chips, chunks, and slivers of stone to fly away. The hammers were made of dolerite, basalt, or wood, the latter having conical-shaped heads. Continuing to chisel their way downward, the workers eventually freed the rough-hewn block. This process was made a bit easier with the introduction of iron wedges at the end of the first millennium B.C. (possibly borrowed from the Romans, who had recently taken over Egypt). Noted scholar Eugen Strouhal writes: "A series of grooves were excavated along a marked line and metal wedges driven into them. Then a number of iron chisels were simultaneously struck in[ward, all in] the same direction, which usually caused the whole block to break off clean."[15]

The next step was to transport the freestanding stone block to the work site. Most or all the men in a gang surrounded the stone and, aided by wooden levers, employed their combined muscle power to load the block onto a wooden sledge (which looked like a big sled). Then, using ropes attached to the front of the sledge, they dragged the block out of the quarry. In the case of Khufu's enormous pyramid, the men did not have to drag the heavily weighted sledge very far, because most of the stones for that monument came from a quarry right on the Giza plateau. In contrast, when a construction site lay many

The Pharaoh Strikes a Deal

When the pharaoh Ramesses II began work on a new city, called Pi-Ramesse, he persuaded thousands of his subjects to help build it by offering them a deal. In exchange for their labor, he would give them certain benefits. An inscription containing some of the wording of this deal was found and reads:

Y ou chosen workmen [and] craftsmen in valuable stone, experienced in [working with] granite . . . good fellows, tireless and vigilant at work all day, who execute their tasks with energy and ability! [I will give you] abundant provisions [in exchange for your labors]. . . . I am your constant provider. The supplies assigned for you are weightier [worth more] than the work, in my desire to [generously] nourish and foster you! I know your labors to be eager and able, and that work is only a pleasure with a full stomach. . . . I have filled the stores for you with . . . bread, meat, cakes [and] sandals, clothing, [and much more]. None of you need [to] pass the night moaning about poverty!

Quoted in K.A. Kitchen. *Pharaoh Triumphant: The Life and Times of Ramesses II.* Cairo: American University in Cairo Press, 1982, p. 120.

miles from the quarry, the workers saved time and effort by loading the stones onto big wooden rafts and floating them down the Nile.

By the time the stone blocks reached the worksite, they had been divided into two groups. In the larger group were the blocks destined for use in foundations or interior sections of the structure. Their surfaces could remain rough because they would be hidden from view in the finished pyramid, temple, or other building. In comparison, the blocks in the second group, whose surfaces *would* be visible, needed to be dressed, or smoothed and

refined. This was accomplished by artisans called masons using various tools, including chisels, saws, and handheld hunks of sandstone.

The goal was to make the surfaces of these stones as smooth as possible, so while dressing a stone a mason periodically tested the degree of flatness. He did this by covering a board with red paint and pressing the board up against the surface of the block. The paint would stick to and thereby reveal any protruding areas, which the mason would then saw and sand again.

With some minor variations, these were the chief methods of readying the stone blocks that were used in erecting ancient Egypt's architectural marvels. The most imposing examples of that nation's several superbly executed arts, they include some of the largest buildings raised in premodern times. Largest of all are the Pyramids, which, because of their enormity and fame, will be examined first.

Wonders of the World: The Great Pyramids

"Of all the countries I have visited," the twelfth-century Iraqi Muslim traveler Abdul Latif remarked,

> there are none that can compare with Egypt for its antiquities [ancient artifacts]. The pyramids are one of the[se] wonders. They have engaged the attention of a multitude of writers who have given in their works the description and dimensions of these edifices. . . . The number of them is three, and they stand in a line at Giza . . . at a short distance apart, their angles pointing to each other and to the east.[16]

Most of the accounts penned by the "multitude" of writers and poets Latif mentions are now lost. Among the few such documents written before his time that *have* survived are those of the fifth-century-B.C. Greek historian Herodotus; the first-century-B.C. Greek historian Diodorus Siculus; Diodorus's contemporary, the Greek geographer Strabo; the first-century-A.D. Roman scholar Pliny the Elder; a chronicler for the ninth-century caliph of Baghdad, Al Mamun; and the tenth-century Arab geographer and traveler Abu al Masudi. All of these accounts agreed with Latif's, as well as with the many European ones that followed—that these monuments at Giza deserved both attention and high praise. Diodorus perhaps offered the best concise comment when he said that the three structures "fill the beholder with wonder and astonishment."[17]

It was not just the immense size of the Giza monuments and other large pyramids dotting Egypt's countryside that evoked feelings of awe. Beginning with the late ancient writers, all of the foreign visitors who saw these edifices agreed that there was a sense of mystery about them. Indeed, for a long time no one knew exactly why or how they were built. Pliny, for example, wrote, "No trace of the method of building these pyramids remains. The most significant problem is how the blocks were raised to such a great height."[18] Many later writers echoed him, and today various mystical theories still surround the Egyptian pyramids. Among others, these include that they possess magical properties, that they were

The Great Pyramids of Giza still awe visitors, much as they must have entranced the people in ancient times.

built by aliens instead of the Egyptians, and that they were erected more than twelve thousand (rather than forty-six hundred) years ago using hidden technology.

The Most Famous Pyramids

The reality is that almost all of the so-called mysteries about the Pyramids have no basis in fact. One of the more common assertions frequently repeated in books and TV shows alike—that no one knows how these monuments were constructed—is demonstrably untrue. Working diligently throughout the nineteenth and twentieth centuries, archaeologists were able to determine most of the materials, tools, and techniques involved in their construction. They also confirmed when the Pyramids were built and which pharaohs were entombed in them.

For instance, most of Egypt's pyramids were erected between about 2700 and 1800 B.C. That era overlaps most of the time periods that modern-day historians call the Old Kingdom (around 2686–2181 B.C.) and Middle Kingdom (around 2055–1650 B.C.). By the start of the period in which Egypt reached its height of power—the New Kingdom (around 1550–1069 B.C.)—pyramids were no longer being constructed. Nor were these huge, aging buildings regularly maintained, as they had been in the past. Thieves had stolen the contents of their inner chambers, including hoards of art and other valuables, well before the advent of the New Kingdom. (These crimes motivated the New Kingdom pharaohs to locate their own tombs in secret spots in the Valley of the Kings.)

The pharaohs who built the three Great Pyramids at Giza could not have foreseen such neglect and looting of their royal burial sites. From the largest to the smallest, they were the tombs of Khufu (reigned 2589–2566 B.C.), Khafre (2558–2532 B.C.), and Menkure (2532–2503 B.C.). The three men were part of the same dynasty, or family line of rulers. (They belonged to the Fourth Dynasty.) Khufu's and Khafre's giant pyramid-tombs remained the most impressive and famous ones in Egypt thereafter, mainly because no other pharaoh built a pyramid nearly as large.

Inventing the Pyramid-Tomb

By the time the Giza pyramids were erected, the form and tradition of the pyramid-tomb was already well-established in Egypt. Before the introduction of this form, kings and other nobles in Egypt had been buried in long, rectangular, flat-topped structures now called mastabas (from an Arabic word meaning "bench"). They were constructed of mud bricks. A typical mastaba, which held some of the deceased's grave goods, stood above ground, while the chambers containing the person's remains and other grave goods were located underground. These chambers grew more extensive as time went on. Also, the government eventually concluded that the mud bricks, which eroded rapidly from the effects of rain and wind, had to be repaired or replaced too often. Moreover, the bricks were too easy for thieves to tunnel through and steal the valuable articles inside.

These problems were at least temporarily overcome by the brilliant architect-builder Imhotep, vizier to the pharaoh Djoser, the second ruler of the Old Kingdom. Scholar Desmond Stewart tells how Imhotep began with a mastaba and ended up single-handedly inventing the pyramid-tomb:

> His first innovation was to construct a mastaba that was not oblong, but square. His second concerned the material from which it was built. [In the past], brick had been used for all buildings. . . . Imhotep decided to dress a core of Saqqara limestone with an outer casing of the superior stone from the quarries on the east bank of the Nile. The mastaba was 26 feet in height and its sides were 207 feet long. [Dissatisfied], Imhotep then extended his great square by about fourteen feet on all sides. The extension was two feet lower than the original mastaba, so that a two-step structure now existed. This may have given [him] his next idea for an improvement. This was to enlarge the base and impose three diminishing squares on [top of] it to form a four-step pyramid. This still did not satisfy Imhotep or his

royal patron, and the original four-step building was soon concealed inside a far more ambitious design—a great step pyramid of six platforms rising to a flat summit just over two hundred feet above ground level.[19]

Inspired by Djoser's step pyramid, later pharaohs built their own versions, each made of durable stone. Also, following Imhotep's design, each pyramid consisted essentially of six large mastabas, each somewhat smaller than the last, piled atop one another. In time, however, builders eliminated the wide indentations making up the steps. They did this by filling them in with extra stone blocks, while more blocks were added to the top, too, which now came to a point. This new approach brought about the first smooth-sided, or "true," pyramid. True pyramids were extremely popular among the rulers of the Fourth Dynasty. Indeed, the dynasty's first pharaoh, Sneferu, built several true pyramids. His son, Khufu, and grandson, Khafre, later constructed their own pyramids, significantly surpassing Sneferu's in the size department.

Before the beginning of the pyramid era, Egyptian kings and nobles were buried in long, rectangular, flat-topped structures called mastabas.

Djoser, Imhotep, and the pharaohs and architects that succeeded them did not experiment so extensively with the pyramidal shape simply by chance. Rather, they were fascinated by it for some deeply spiritual reasons related to the unique Egyptian vision of the heavens, royalty, and afterlife. First, they believed that there had existed a primeval (very ancient) mound of creation—the *benben*. According to their mythology, this sacred hill was shaped like a pyramid. They also saw the pyramidal shape as the symbol, or representation, of an invisible stairway, or ramp, that started at the earth's surface and rose up into the heavens. Following a pharaoh's death, his soul supposedly used the sacred ramp to make its way into the sky and there commune with the gods. An excerpt from the Pyramid Texts, the earliest known Egyptian funerary writings, reads:

> He [the pharaoh] has leapt skyward as a grasshopper [would]. He ascends into the sky among his brethren, the gods. . . . A ramp to the sky is built for him, that he may go up to the sky [on it]. He goes up upon the smoke of the great exhalation [divine breath]. He flies

Pharaoh Djoser's architect-builder Imhotep took the structure of a mastaba to a new level, turning it into a step pyramid.

as a bird, and he settles as a beetle on the empty seat on the ship of Ra [the sun god]. . . . He has gone up into the sky and has found Ra [and] has taken his stand with Ra in the northern part of the sky.[20]

From Foundation to Casing Stones

Modern-day visitors to the Giza plateau can easily visualize the Great Pyramids as stepping stones toward the heavens. Indeed, for many years those visitors routinely climbed up the stone blocks, whose levels do resemble large steps leading upward. However, people could not have climbed up the Pyramids in that manner during the initial centuries following their completion. This was because each was originally encased in a layer of smooth stone having no footholds whatsoever. The way this was done becomes clear when one considers the step-by-step process by which these structures were erected.

The first step was to level the base, or foundation. If it was not perfectly level, the building's tremendous weight—in the millions of tons—would not be evenly distributed. In that case there would be a slow but steady shifting of the weight that would lead to cracking, crumbling, and eventually collapse. The fact that Khufu's pyramid has endured so long is in part a testament to the care the builders lavished in creating a level foundation. Indeed, the difference in flatness from one side of the monument to the other is only 0.75 inches (2 cm). This is an amazing degree of uniformity in a structure so large and built without the aid of machines.

As for how this tremendous accuracy was achieved, the current consensus among experts is that the workers first drove a series of wooden stakes into the ground. To these they attached long cords running horizontally to mark where the upper surface of the stone foundation should be. To make sure the placement of the cords would create a perfectly flat base, they used a plumb line. This is a rod from which a small weight (the plumb bob) hangs on a string. Because the weight always points toward the earth's center, the string attached to it is vertical. So by seeing that a horizontal string met the vertical string at a right angle, the builders confirmed that the horizontal string was flat rather than tilted at an angle. After this was done, the workers laid down the stones one row at a time. As they did so, they checked and rechecked the height of each block, adjusting its level if necessary. (A few experts still hold to an older theory, which speculates that the flat base was achieved by flooding trenches surrounding the foundation with water and matching the tops of the stones to the water's level.)

Older Theory for Leveling the Site

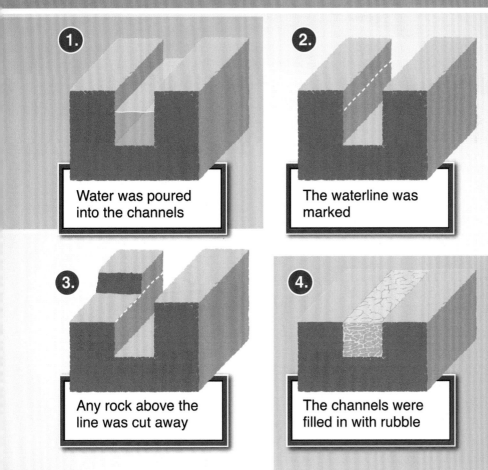

1. Water was poured into the channels

2. The waterline was marked

3. Any rock above the line was cut away

4. The channels were filled in with rubble

When the sturdy foundation of Khufu's tomb was in place, the builders began adding one layer, or course, after another of stone blocks to create the pyramid's body. Each block weighed an average of 2.5 tons (2.27t). (Some located in the structure's interior are considerably heavier that that.) Laying in the stones for the first and lowest course was fairly easily accomplished by moving them on thick wooden rollers. But raising the rest of the estimated total of 2.3 million blocks upward to form higher and higher courses was much more difficult. The

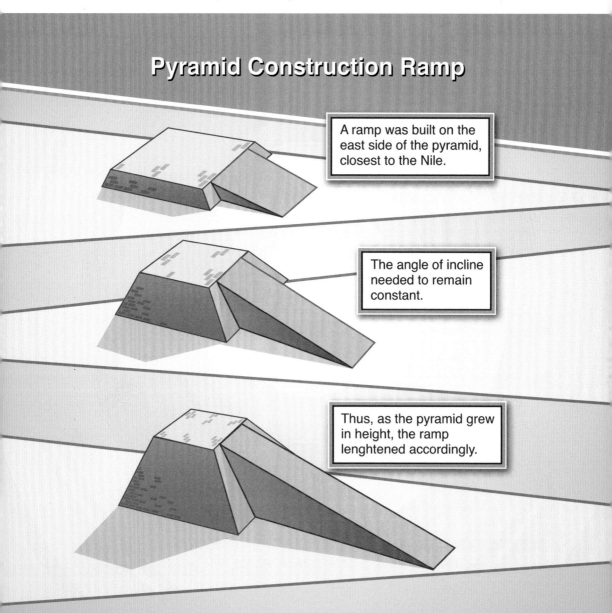

Pyramid Construction Ramp

A ramp was built on the east side of the pyramid, closest to the Nile.

The angle of incline needed to remain constant.

Thus, as the pyramid grew in height, the ramp lenghtened accordingly.

HOW MANY WORKERS DOES IT TAKE TO BUILD A PYRAMID?

One question often posed to archaeologists and historians is, how many people were needed to erect a giant pyramid? The Greek historian Herodotus, who visited Egypt in the fifth century B.C., suggested that one hundred thousand workers toiled to build Khufu's pyramid-tomb. However, a majority of modern-day experts feel that that figure is far too high. Some very strong evidence for this comes from Harvard University scholar and noted Egyptologist Mark Lehner. In the 1990s he conducted an experiment that was documented by the distinguished TV science program *NOVA*. In the test, a group of twelve volunteers temporarily transformed themselves into ancient Egyptian pyramid workers. They lived in primitive shelters in the desert, labored in a quarry, went barefoot, and used no modern tools or devices. In the space of twenty-one days, these men quarried 186 stone blocks. They then put in more days dragging the stones and setting them in rows, as if they were the first course of a pyramid. From the accomplishments of the twelve men, Lehner made a rough estimate of the number of workers required to erect Khufu's pyramid. The answer was that five thousand or fewer men could have done it in twenty years, or ten thousand or fewer men could have done it in ten years.

manner in which the workers did this has been debated by scholars and nonscholars alike for a long time and is still somewhat unclear.

One theory is that the builders piled up large, gradually rising ramps or mounds of sand and stone debris and dragged the sledges holding the blocks up the ramps. Numerous different shapes of and configurations for these ramps have been proposed. One of the more credible suggestions is that there was a ramp on each of a pyramid's four sides. In whatever way the ramps, if any, were placed, they were obviously removed after the last courses of stones were in place.

It is possible that such ramps were used in the building of at least some of Egypt's larger pyramids. But even if that is true, most scholars think they worked in conjunction with other methods. Several suggestions for these techniques have been advanced, including some involving wooden levers to lift the blocks from one course to the next.

One ingenious suggestion that has become popular in recent years is that of English master builder Peter Hodges. He did experiments with a 2-ton test load (1.8t) and found that two men could lever up one end of it and place wooden blocks beneath it. When they did the same thing on the opposite side, the load now rested evenly on the blocks and had been raised several inches. They repeated this process a few more times until they had raised the load by an amount equal to the height of a typical stone in Khufu's pyramid.

Now imagine if the same approach was used after the first layer of stones had been dragged into position above the pyramid's foundation. Call that layer "course A." Using the levers, two or three men could raise a block from the foundation level to the top of course A. Several such teams would work simultaneously on the structure's perimeter, raising blocks and moving them into place to form the next layer, "course B." Then the teams would raise new blocks. They would first lift them from the foundation level to the open outer edge of course A. Then they would raise them to the top of course B. These new stones would be used to create "course C," and the process would be continuously repeated, causing the monument to rise higher and higher.

This method or one similar to it is credible because it is simple and energy efficient. In contrast, erecting giant earthen ramps, though possible, requires a lot of time and an enormous amount of energy. Another factor that makes Hodges's approach believable is that it closely matches the one described by Herodotus. After his visit to Egypt, the ancient historian reported:

Lifting the Stones

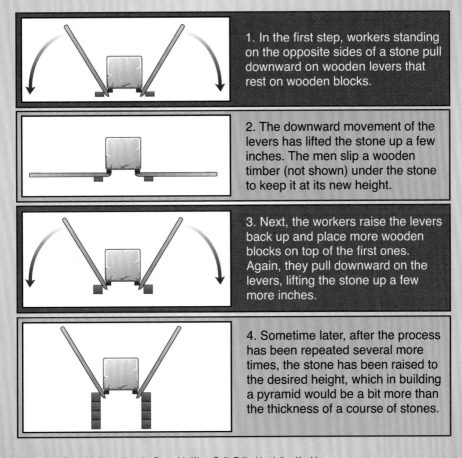

1. In the first step, workers standing on the opposite sides of a stone pull downward on wooden levers that rest on wooden blocks.

2. The downward movement of the levers has lifted the stone up a few inches. The men slip a wooden timber (not shown) under the stone to keep it at its new height.

3. Next, the workers raise the levers back up and place more wooden blocks on top of the first ones. Again, they pull downward on the levers, lifting the stone up a few more inches.

4. Sometime later, after the process has been repeated several more times, the stone has been raised to the desired height, which in building a pyramid would be a bit more than the thickness of a course of stones.

Taken from: Peter Hodges, *How the Pyramids Were Built*. Edited by Julian Keable. Warminster, UK: Aris and Phillips, 1993.

The method employed was to build [the pyramid] in steps, or, as some call them, tiers or terraces. When the base was complete, the blocks for the first tier above it were lifted from the ground level by contrivances [levers] made of short timbers. On this first tier there was another, which raised the blocks a stage higher, then yet another which raised them higher still. Each tier, or story, had its set of levers. Or it may be that they used the same one, which, being easy to carry, they shifted up from stage to stage as soon as its load was dropped into place.[21]

The Bent Pyramid at Dashur still shows some of the casing stones that covered the structure.

Whatever method or combination of methods was employed to raise the stones, when all of the latter were in place, the final step was to add the casing stones. These consisted of pieces of smooth, white limestone that completely encased the structure, giving it a flat, solid, polished, and highly attractive outer surface. As anyone who has seen photos of the Pyramids knows, these stones no longer exist. Thieves stripped them off during medieval and early modern times to use them for building smaller structures.

Art by and for the People

With their casing stones gleaming in the bright midday sun, the recently built Giza pyramids were not only stunning, impressive sights. They were also architectural marvels and magnificent works of art. Khufu's monument (then called *Akhet-Khufu*, or "Khufu's Horizon") stood 481 feet (147m) high, making it by far the tallest human-made structure in the world. (That record was destined to remain untouched until the French erected their own architectural marvel, the Eiffel Tower, in 1889.) Towering nearby, Khafre's pyramid stood 478 feet (146m) high. Although considerably smaller, at 220 feet (67m) high, Menkure's tomb was still taller than Djoser's Step Pyramid at Saqqara.

It was not merely the great size of these buildings that made them exciting to their ancient builders. The fact that their interiors bore the burial chambers of their supposedly semidivine kings was also inspiring to Egyptians of all walks of life. They were, after all, one of the most devoutly religious

TRYING TO DETER TOMB ROBBERS

One of the great challenges faced by the builders of ancient Egypt's pyramid-tombs was finding a way to keep grave robbers from looting these monuments of their precious grave goods. Over time, the designers came up with a number of security measures. One consisted of placing three thick stone doors, one directly behind another, at the entrance to the inner burial chamber. In theory, that would keep the thieves out. A second measure was to devise a system that filled the corridor outside the burial chamber with enormous stone blocks during the sealing of the tomb. A dramatic scene in the finale of the 1955 movie *Land of the Pharaohs* shows such a system sealing the corridors of Khufu's pyramid. (The scene also depicts the pharaoh's high priests and queen trapped inside, doomed to starve and die, which did not actually happen.) Another line of defense was to insert a polished casing stone over the outer entrance to the tomb's interior. That way, hopefully, the tomb robbers would be unable to figure out where the entrance was. Finally, the tomb builders placed guards around the tomb. However, all of these security measures ultimately failed. The vast majority of Egypt's ancient tombs were eventually penetrated and robbed of their valuables.

peoples in history. In their minds, these tombs not only held the mummified royal bodies, but were also the launching pads, so to speak, for the ascent of the pharaohs' souls into the sky. In the words of scholars Kevin Jackson and Jonathan Stamp, to an ancient Egyptian a pyramid-tomb was "a machine for resurrection." The building's interior was "an ingenious machine indeed, made up of chambers, antechambers, open passages, hidden passages, shafts, and [sliding doors]."[22]

In Khufu's pyramid, the most crucial of these interior spaces was the King's Chamber. Measuring 34 feet (10m) long, 17 feet (5m) wide, and 19 feet (5.7m) high, it held the stone

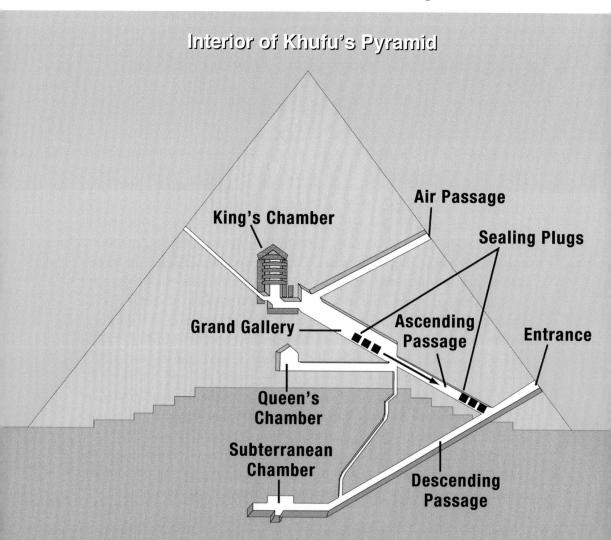

Interior of Khufu's Pyramid

coffin bearing the pharaoh's mummy. The rest of the chamber was filled to the brim with food, clothing, chariots, boats, and all manner of beautiful artistic treasures. This alone made the pyramid an extremely sacred place.

The monument also had great religious significance because of the way it and the other pyramids were aligned on the Giza plateau. They were positioned in such a way that the four sides of each structure pointed directly toward the four cardinal points—north, east, south, and west. Also, the official entrances to these buildings were placed in the middle of their north faces. This may have been done so that the kings' souls would meet up with the gods in the northern sector of the sky. The positioning of the Pyramids would therefore ensure that the deceased pharaohs had a direct, unhindered passageway to their divine fates. Thus, these timeless structures were a unique example of grand art created by a national effort and for an ultimate goal that virtually every person in society deeply cared about.

3

Palaces to Pylons: Egypt's Monumental Arts

T he huge pyramid-tombs that held the remains of ancient Egypt's pharaohs are so famous and so often written about that some people know little or nothing about that nation's other works of monumental architecture. These other works were both numerous and masterly in design and execution. They ranged from large palaces in which the kings oversaw splendid ceremonial functions; to massive temples dedicated to the gods; to the towering, tapering stone needles known as obelisks; to military fortresses so enormous that an entire town could fit inside; to a lighthouse taller than the first modern skyscrapers and so well built that it lasted more than fifteen centuries.

A great many of these immense artistic marvels were created during the roughly five-hundred-year-long New Kingdom, when Egypt was at its richest, strongest, and most influential. As architectural achievements, they were no less amazing than the Pyramids of the Old and Middle kingdoms. This is because Egypt's technology progressed at the proverbial snail's pace. Indeed, despite the passage of many centuries, the builders of the New Kingdom were not significantly more advanced than those of the Old Kingdom. The "New Kingdom structures were

tremendous feats," the late historian Lionel Casson wrote. "Yet during the whole period of Egyptian engineering, from the first stone building put up by Imhotep about 2700 B.C. to [the pharaoh] Ramesses' [giant] structures fifteen hundred years later, the same primitive tools and methods were used."[23]

Palaces and Royal Mansions

The construction methods used to erect these buildings may have been basic. But the edifices themselves were complex and visually stunning. The royal palaces were certainly meant to evoke beauty and grandeur, for it was within them that the pharaohs led various religious and social ceremonies and met with foreign ambassadors. To make a king's religious duties and rituals easier to perform, the palaces were often attached directly to temples by means of a covered passageway.

A Dam to Battle the Floods

Among the many massive structures created by the ancient Egyptian kings were dams. None have survived intact. But references to them appear in surviving ancient documents. The first Egyptian pharaoh, Narmer, also called Min, was said to have erected a large dam. In his history book, the fifth-century-B.C. Greek historian Herodotus recounted what some Egyptian priests told him about Min's dam:

When the Nile overflows, the whole country is converted into a sea, and the towns, which alone remain above water, look like islands. . . . The priests told me that it was Min, the first king of Egypt, who raised the dam which protects Memphis from the floods. The river used to flow along the base of the sandy hills [to the west], and this monarch, by damming it up . . . drained the original channel and diverted it to a new one half way between the two lines of hills. To this day, the elbow which the Nile forms here . . . is most carefully watched by the [local rulers], who strengthen the dam every year. For should the river burst it, Memphis might be completely overwhelmed.

Herodotus. *The Histories*. Translated by Aubrey de Sélincourt. New York: Penguin, 2003, p. 165.

Another important aspect of the connection between palace and temple was the so-called window of appearance. According to Egyptologist Rosalie David, this was

a wide, open balcony that overlooked the street where the king and his family showed themselves to the people. The balcony was lavishly decorated with gold [and other valuable materials] and provided a place from which the king could inspect the [gifts] piled up below and . . . was also the place where he could hand out honors [to] various courtiers as a mark of recognition for their services and achievements.[24]

In most cases, the kings and their families did not actually live in the part of the palace where such ceremonies took place, as Roman emperors and European monarchs later did. Egypt's royal family lived either in a separate wing of a palace or in a completely detached mansion nearby. This wing or mansion was called the *per-aa*, or "great house."

Evidence shows that Egypt's palaces were not only monumental structures with many rooms and corridors, but also expensively and elegantly decorated. That made them works of art in and of themselves, as is France's one-time royal abode, the magnificent Louvre (now a museum). However, the palaces were among only a few of the large-scale Egyptian buildings not fashioned of durable stone. Instead, both palaces and royal mansions were typically made of mud bricks reinforced by timber beams. Because these materials readily disintegrate over time, none of the Egyptian palaces survived into modern times.

Cult and Mortuary Temples

The temples that connected with the royal palaces were known as cult temples, one of several distinct categories of temple in ancient Egypt. Whatever their type or purpose, literally hundreds of temples existed there at any given time. This is not surprising, given Herodotus's famous remark—that the Egyptians "are religious to excess, beyond any other nation in the world."[25]

Of the diverse varieties of Egyptian temples, those labeled "cult" and "mortuary" were by far the most common. Cult temples were the ones in which direct worship of one or more gods occurred. (Today the term *cult* conjures up images of brainwashed individuals doing the bidding of a twisted, antisocial fanatic. But in ancient times a cult was a congregation of worshippers of a specific god, plus its temples, priests, and holy objects.) Early Egyptian cult temples were varied in design and

An inner shrine flanked by huge columns in the Temple of Horus. Stone temples had become the standard by the time of the New Kingdom.

made of a blend of mud bricks, timber beams, and stone. Most survive in an advanced state of ruin.

By contrast, several New Kingdom cult temples have survived in fairly good condition because they were built mainly of stone. Also, the design, or style, of cult temples in the New Kingdom became more or less standard (with occasional exceptions) and continued into later periods. Distinguished Egyptologists Ian Shaw and Paul Nicholson describe this standard layout for cult temples, saying that the key component was

> the innermost cult-chamber or shrine, where the image of the deity was kept. The activities of the temple revolved around the worship and celebration of the deity's cult via the image in the shrine, and the building itself was not a meeting-place for worshipers. A series of

processional [walk]ways passed through open court-yards, hypostyle halls [interior chambers], and massive ceremonial gateways, through which the king and his priests could gradually approach the cult image. . . . The backdrop for religious festivals . . . usually consisted of the transportation of the deity's statue, carried in a bark [boat-shaped platform], from one temple to another. [26]

The hypostyle halls mentioned above were common features of Egyptian architecture, especially in temples. Such a hall consisted of a massive chamber or covered courtyard in which the ceiling was supported by many rows of thick, sturdy columns. Both the columns and the walls were beautifully decorated with paintings and sometimes sculptures, making the chamber a superb synthesis of different artistic mediums.

The other major temple type, the mortuary temple (called *hwt*, or "mansion"), was not a place for worshipping a deity. Instead, its purpose was to provide spiritual assistance for the soul of a king or queen. Such a structure was most often erected near the royal person's burial site, and the priests who worked in the temple prayed and made offerings intended to nourish and sustain the deceased's spirit in the afterlife.

One of the finest and better preserved of the New Kingdom mortuary temples is Medinet Habu, in central Egypt, built for the pharaoh Ramesses III, who reigned from 1184 to 1153 B.C. From the outside in, it begins with a lavishly decorated entranceway opening into a large courtyard. Next comes another ornate entranceway that leads into a second courtyard, which itself opens into a gigantic hypostyle hall with a veritable forest of columns. In its heyday, the hall had a chapel and other sacred chambers to the rear of the structure.

Pylons and Obelisks

Each of the entranceways in Medinet Habu and numerous other Egyptian temples was fronted by a handsome architectural feature called a pylon. According to archaeologist Steven Snape, it consisted of a relatively modestly sized gateway flanked by two massive stone towers. The pylon was doubtless intended to be an impressive and intimidating entrance [to a temple or other building and] also served as a convenient permanent billboard for royal propaganda. This might [consist of a generalized scene of] the king smiting his enemies or a [depiction of] a more specific [battle]. In front of the pylon stood examples of giant "temple furniture," especially tall monolithic obelisks and colossal seated or standing statues of the king.[27]

The pylons and their warlike propaganda were intended not only to trumpet the pharaoh's power and bravery, but also to fend off the forces of evil and chaos. Another ritualistic function of a pylon was related to its shape. Each of its flat-topped towers looked like the hieroglyph known as the *akhet*, which symbolized the horizon, or dividing line between earth and sky. So a pylon was seen as the horizon between the disordered, dangerous outer world and the safe and peaceful sanctuary within the temple.

The pylons of Ramesses III commemorate his victory over the Sea Peoples during his reign. Pylons were often used as propaganda tools.

A ROMAN DESCRIBES AN EGYPTIAN OBELISK

In this passage from his Natural History, *the first-century-A.D. Roman scholar Pliny the Elder describes an obelisk erected by the New Kingdom pharaoh Ramesses II. The highly exaggerated number of workers mentioned and the supposed involvement of the king's son smack of fable and demonstrate how little factual information about the building methods employed had survived by Pliny's time.*

[The obelisk] is 200 feet in height and is extraordinarily thick, each side being 17 feet in width. Some 120,000 men are said to have carried out this work. When the obelisk was about to be set upright, the king himself was afraid that the lifting equipment would not be strong enough to take the weight. To make his workmen pay attention to the dangers, he tied his son to the top, so that in ensuring the child's safety, the work-force would treat the monolith with necessary care.

Pliny the Elder. *Natural History: A Selection.* Translated by John F. Healy. New York: Penguin, 1991, pp. 349–350.

Snape mentions tall obelisks standing in front of a pylon. A towering stone needle with a top resembling that of a pyramid, an obelisk could appear not only as part of a pair, but also singly. It was used for decoration and also possessed religious and astrological significance.

In particular, the resemblance of an obelisk's peak to that of a pyramid made it another symbol for the sacred *benben*, or original mound of creation. An obelisk's apex was meant to catch and reflect the rising sun each morning in the same manner that the *benben* had supposedly captured the beams of the world's first sunrise at the dawn of time. To better reflect the sun, an obelisk's top was covered with sheets of copper or bronze. Builders sometimes enhanced this visual effect by constructing an obelisk from Aswan granite. That kind of stone has a distinctive pinkish hue that adds extra color to reflected sunlight.

Obelisks varied in height, about 70 feet (22m) or so being average. Not surprisingly, they were also very heavy. The two raised in the temple complex at Karnak by Queen Hatshepsut weigh a whopping 323 tons (293t) each. One of the obelisks erected by her successor, Thutmose III, which now stands in Rome, Italy, weighs 455 tons (413t). Another of Thutmose's obelisks, which was never finished because it developed a large crack during the quarrying phase, would have weighed an incredible 1,168 tons (1,060t).

A Military Art

No less impressive than temples and obelisks and even more connected to warfare than pylons were Egypt's enormous frontier fortresses. Among the more striking engineering accomplishments that nation ever produced, they were designed to keep out enemies who might threaten the supposedly superior civilization the Egyptians felt they had created. (They viewed all other nations and peoples as, to one degree or another, less civilized than themselves.) During the New Kingdom, when Egypt built an empire by conquering neighboring lands, the fortresses also became weapons depots and rest stops for armies leaving for and returning from those lands.

The earliest Egyptian fortifications were defensive walls built around individual towns, much like those in Mesopotamia and other ancient regions. Over time, the tops of these walls became crenellated. That is, they had stone notches alternating with open spaces, just like those in medieval castles. (Soldiers hid behind the notches and fired arrows or other weapons through the open spaces.)

Similar walls were later erected around military camps near Egypt's borders, thereby creating the first of the country's fortresses. At first built of mud bricks, these structures eventually featured solid stone walls up to 40 feet (12m) high, taller than a modern four-story building. Such a fortress was not composed simply of a few plain, straight walls, however. These

buildings became increasingly complex, well thought out, architecturally balanced, and even visually attractive. This likely derived from the Egyptians' love for large-scale edifices like their religiously inspired pyramids and temples. As Ian Shaw says, "The distinct features of Egyptian [fortresses], with their symmetrical and often elegant designs, probably reflect the monumental traditions of Egyptian religious architecture just as much as [practical] military requirements."[28]

Although some variations existed, the typical layout of the interior of a fortress featured a well-ordered grid of streets lined with soldiers' barracks, officers' quarters, workshops, and storehouses. A wider road ran around the townlike complex of streets and buildings, separating them from the imposing defensive walls. Meanwhile, below ground and out of sight were several well-built secret tunnels for bringing in water from the nearest river or lake and providing an emergency escape route.

The best-preserved and most impressive ancient Egyptian fortress is Buhen, built on the west bank of the Nile during the New Kingdom era.

TWO GREAT ROYAL ARCHITECTS

The names of very few ancient Egyptian architects have survived, and of those that have, little is known about those individuals. This was certainly the case with the architects Senenmut and Amenhotep. Senenmut was said to have been the master builder for Queen Hatshepsut. His masterpiece was her mortuary temple at Deir el-Bahri, near the entrance to the Valley of the Kings. Having a unique design that features rows of columns similar to those in a Greek temple, it was one of the most imposing and beautiful buildings of the ancient world and remains largely intact. Senenmut also built a tomb for his parents, which was discovered in the 1930s. A carving in it shows him standing alone with his mother and father, which some experts think indicates he was unmarried. Other fragmentary clues suggest that he was Hatshepsut's lover.

Amenhotep lived about a century after Senenmut. Chief architect and builder for the pharaoh Amenhotep III (1390–1352 B.C., and no relation to his architect), Amenhotep also organized all the laborers in Egypt for that ruler. His supreme achievement was the pharaoh's mortuary temple in Thebes. Long after his death, the architect Amenhotep, like his eminent predecessor Imhotep, was hailed as a great healer and thinker.

Hatshepsut's mortuary temple was built by the renowned Egyptian architect Senenmut.

The best-preserved and in many ways most impressive ancient Egyptian fortress is at Buhen, on the Nile's west bank in what was then the neighboring land of Nubia (which Egypt often controlled). As Shaw describes it:

> The grandiose defenses included an outer enclosure wall over 700 meters long and 4 meters thick! The wall was strengthened at intervals by 32 semicircular [towers]. The western wall had five large towers as well as a huge central tower which functioned as the main gateway to the site. This entrance [eventually measured] 47 by 30 meters. Both outer and inner defenses were surrounded by ditches following the outline of the walls.[29]

To give some idea of the titanic dimensions of this structure, it could easily have held three pyramids the size of Khufu's within its walls! Moreover, the largest army and collection of siege machines ever assembled in medieval Europe (before the introduction of cannons) could not have breached Buhen's walls. That fortress and others similar to it made up a kind of military art form that few peoples in history had the organization, industry, patience, and sheer will to construct.

The Model for Ancient Lighthouses

Still another architectural marvel produced by the industrious Egyptians was the famous lighthouse at Alexandria (located in the Nile's delta). Like Khufu's pyramid, the lighthouse, named the Pharos after the island on which it stood, made the famous list of the seven ancient wonders. To say the Egyptians erected the lighthouse is accurate insomuch as most of the masons, sculptors, carpenters, and laborers were local residents. However, its designer was almost certainly Greek. This is because the Pharos was built in the 290s and 280s B.C., when Egypt was ruled by the Ptolemaic dynasty. The first Ptolemy (TAW-luh-mee) had been a high-ranking officer under Alexander the Great, the Macedonian Greek general who had taken over

Egypt more than three decades before. When Alexander died, Ptolemy seized the country himself and founded the Greek ruling family that would later produce the legendary Cleopatra VII.

As for who the Greek architect was, modern-day experts are uncertain. One likely candidate was a member of Ptolemy's royal court named Sostratus, although he may only have helped to finance the structure. Whoever the designer was, he and his Egyptian artisans created one of history's most beautiful buildings. The Pharos, which rose along the outer rim of Alexandria's harbor, had three main sections, or tiers, each sitting atop another. The lowest and largest tier was 197 feet

The Pharos, a lighthouse in Alexandria built in the third century B.C., stood until an earthquake destroyed it in the early 1300s. It was the last great structure the Egyptians would build.

(60m) high. The second tier was 98 feet (30m) high, and the third and uppermost tier was 26 feet (8m) high and held the fireplace that provided the beacon for sailors out at sea. The Pharos's total height, counting a statue standing at the top, was 344 feet (105m), as tall as a modern thirty-seven- or thirty-eight-story skyscraper.

Made of various kinds and grades of stone, the Pharos was built to last, and it did. At first it became the model for most of the lighthouses constructed across the Mediterranean world in the centuries that followed. According to Pliny the Elder, "Similar beacons [that copied its style] now burn brightly in several places, for example at Ostia [Rome's port] and Ravenna [in northeastern Italy]."[30] The great lighthouse outlived not only the Ptolemies and Pliny, but also the Roman Empire and even the Norman invasion of Britain in 1066. A mosaic created for Saint Mark's Cathedral in Venice in about 1200 depicted the Pharos, showing that it was then still mostly intact. As near as historians can tell, this majestic structure, one of the greatest examples of ancient architectural prowess, was finally destroyed by earthquakes in the early 1300s. In this way a significant piece of ancient Egyptian art met its end.

Meanwhile, other examples of Egypt's splendid architectural wonders survived to the present. The mighty monuments at Giza, which were already ancient when Herodotus saw them, continue to draw crowds of visitors from across the globe each year. There is no way to know if King Khufu's soul achieved immortality, as he hoped it would. But his towering tomb appears to be well on its way to achieving that goal.

Statues and Reliefs: The Art of Stone Sculpture

> I met a traveler from an antique land
> Who said: Two vast and trunkless legs of stone
> Stand in the desert. Near them on the sand,
> Half sunk, a shattered visage lies.

So begins a famous nineteenth-century ode by England's great poet Percy Bysshe Shelley. The legs and visage (face or head) he mentions belonged to a statue of an ancient king whom Shelley calls Ozymandias. More is said about that long-dead ruler in the poem's haunting finale:

> On the pedestal these words appear:
> "My name is Ozymandias, King of Kings.
> Look on my works, ye mighty, and despair!"
> Nothing beside remains. Round the decay
> Of that colossal wreck, boundless and bare,
> The lone and level sands stretch far away.[31]

Although no Egyptian king bore the name *Ozymandias* per se, Shelley based him on a real pharaoh. The name was a mangled translation of one of the throne names of the New Kingdom ruler Ramesses II (reigned 1279–1213 B.C.), one of Egypt's most prolific builders. The poet knew that Ramesses had erected numerous giant statues, or colossi, of himself. Among these was one that stood 62 feet (19m) high and weighed an estimated 1,000 tons (907t). Its upper section had collapsed during an earthquake in ancient times, and several Europeans, possibly including Shelley, had seen it lying in the sand.

Shelley's words did more than provide a memorable metaphor for the inevitable impermanence of human rulers and empires. He also called attention to one of ancient Egypt's greatest and most enduring art forms—stone sculpture. Generations of Egyptian sculptors helped to decorate both the insides and outsides of palaces, temples, tombs, and other structures. Some specialized in carving freestanding statues that ranged from modest figurines to huge colossi like those of Ramesses. Others created reliefs (or bas-reliefs), figures and scenes raised three-dimensionally from a flat background. These artistic masterpieces, a number of which have survived, exhibit many aspects of Egyptian society, from sweeping parades and battles to small snapshots of personal life.

One of the many colossal statues of Ramesses II stands in front of the Temple of Amon in Karnak.

Statues as Spiritual Vessels

Modern-day archaeologists and historians have learned a great deal about ancient Egyptian life through examinations of complete and partial statues. The ancient sculptors regularly captured current styles of clothing, shoes, and headdresses, for example. Also, inscriptions on statues or their bases have revealed information about individual rulers and officials, historical events, and social customs. In addition, studying statues and other artifacts has taught scholars why and how these artistic works were carved.

As for why the Egyptians created statues, especially large-scale ones, the primary motivation was not what most people might expect. All ancient peoples carved statues at least in part to depict and honor their gods. But beyond that, each culture viewed the creation of statuary, including depictions of humans and animals, in distinctive ways. Those who are familiar with the ancient Greeks know that in large part they intended such works to be artistic expressions of beauty, love, heroism, despair, and other core human emotions and values.

The Colossi of Memnon sit at the funerary temple of Amenhotep III in Thebes. The colossi were created for specific religious purposes or to invoke symbolic meaning.

The Egyptians had a very different view of most statues, however. The vast majority of their freestanding sculptures, particularly the colossi, were created for specific religious purposes or to evoke a symbolic meaning, usually also spiritual in nature. For instance, statues were most often perceived as receptacles, or host vehicles, for spirits or other nonphysical beings. Furthermore, the beings who inhabited such sculptures expected living people to acknowledge them and provide them with various ritual offerings. British Egyptologist Gay Robins explains:

> Most statues were places where a non-physical entity—a deity [or] spirits of the dead—could manifest [take up a presence or residence] in this world. The statue provided a physical body and had to be recognizable and appropriate to the being that was meant to manifest in it. . . . Most statues formed a ritual focal point. Offerings were made to them, or rather to the being inhabiting them, incense was burned before them, and the correct words were recited and actions performed. In order for the statue to function this way, it had to undergo [a ritual known as] "the opening of the mouth" . . . which vitalized [animated] it and enabled it to house the being it represented.[32]

Because the sculpture was seen as the spirit's vessel and was expected to resemble him, her, or it, sculptors did their best to capture the physical likenesses of the beings the statues represented. For that reason, Ramesses's many carved stone images bore a definite resemblance to him. In the same way, a well-known sculpture of an earlier New Kingdom ruler, Queen Hatshepsut, provides valuable evidence of her physical attributes.

Liberating Statues from Stone

Among the materials the Egyptian sculptors employed for their statues are metal, wood, and stone. But the majority of the statues that survive are made of stone (including sandstone, limestone, granite, and others). To work these rigid, durable substances, the artists used a wide array of simple but effective tools and techniques. As described by Egyptologist Rosalie David, they included,

> pounding the block [of stone] with a [harder] stone; rubbing it with stones and an abrasive powder; sawing it with a copper blade . . . boring it with a copper tubular drill . . . and drilling it with a copper or stone point. . . . The tubular drill [was made from] a hollow tube of copper that was rolled between the hands or rotated by means of a bow. Another boring tool—the bow drill—consisted of a drill with a wooden handle and a crescent-shaped flint bit that was turned by hand.[33]

As a rule, the block of stone from which a sculptor carved a statue was, as Robins says,

> slightly larger than the desired size of the finished object. Front and back views of the image were sketched out on the front and back of the block, while profile images were drawn on each of the sides. From [about 2000 B.C.] on, these outlines were probably laid out on a squared grid . . . that ran all the way around the block so as to ensure that all the sketches matched up. Sculptors then cut away the stone on all four sides and the top around the sketched outline until they achieved the rough shape of the statue.[34]

Once this rough version of the statue was complete, the artists began to concentrate on detail. They started modeling the facial features, the hair or headdress, and the muscles and clothes of the subject. If it was an animal rather than a person they were depicting, they carved its ears, snout, and eyes, often inlaying the latter with black and white stones. In fact, whether creating a human, god, or animal, the eyes were often rendered with a striking degree of detail and realism. In this phase of the process, the Egyptian artisans "were matchless," historian Lionel Casson remarked. "For ordinary work they were content with inserting an eyeball of crystalline limestone with a piece of obsidian for the iris and pupil. In the best work, there were eyelids of silver or copper, an eyeball of polished quartz, a cornea of rock crystal with a disk of brown resin for the iris, and, in a hole in the center of the iris, a plug of very dark brown or black resin for the pupil."[35]

Another kind of detail the sculptors worked on when carving a statue was the specific pose of the stone or wooden figure. In general, the two principal poses were standing and sitting. (A third pose, kneeling, was far less common.) There were standard conventions for male statues and others for female statues. In a standing male statue, for example, the left leg typically advanced forward of the right. This symbolized masculinity, in the sense that socially speaking a man was seen as being more active, aggressive, and in charge of life than a woman was. Accordingly, it was most common in a female statue for the left leg to advance only slightly in front of the right one. Quite often female figures had both legs together, a pose known as mummiform.

Another convention in carving statues was for a man to carry a staff, which symbolized his authority, especially over his wife and other women. Other conventions pertained to a ruler. When sitting, he or she was depicted on a throne. When standing, a male ruler's statue featured a distinctive forward

This Egyptian fresco depicts a sculptors' workshop and shows the sculptors at various stages of their work.

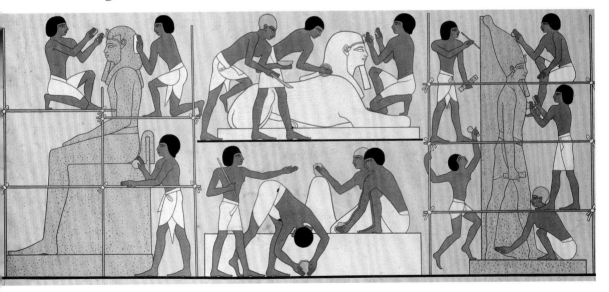

PLINY DESCRIBES THE GREAT SPHINX

In his encyclopedia-like Natural History, *the first-century-A.D. Roman scholar Pliny the Elder said the following about the Great Sphinx at Giza, which was then already about twenty-six hundred years old:*

In front of the pyramids is the Sphinx, which is even more noteworthy [than those monuments]. The local inhabitants worship it as a deity, yet say nothing about it. They believe that King Harmais [a mythical character] is buried inside it and like to think it was transported there [from somewhere else]. It is, however, carved from local rock. The face of this legendary creature is colored red—a mark of reverence. The circumference of its head, at its forehead, is 102 feet; its length, 243 feet; and it measures about 62 feet from its stomach to the top of the asp [stone snake] on its head.

Pliny the Elder. *Natural History: A Selection.* Translated by John F. Healy. New York: Penguin, 1991, p. 352.

By the time the first-century Roman scholar Pliny the Elder described the Great Sphinx in his work Natural History, *it was already twenty-six hundred years old.*

thrust of the left leg, while often one hand carried a scepter, both viewed as signs of one who maintained order in both the nation and the universe.

Human-Animal Hybrids

Still another convention involved the depiction of humans versus animals. Although Egyptian sculptors created images of both people and animals, among their favorite and more frequent subjects were crosses between the two. On the one hand, many of Egypt's traditional gods were regularly depicted with the heads or other features of animals. Statues of the sun god Ra, for instance, frequently had a man's body and a falcon's (or hawk's) head. Similarly, Anubis, god of embalming and the dead, had a jackal's head; Hathor, goddess of love and music, bore a cow's head; and Sobek, deity of the Nile River, had the head of a crocodile.

On the other hand, no less popular among both sculptors and the Egyptians in general was another human-animal hybrid —the sphinx. This mythical beast usually had the body of a lion and the head of a human, most often a man. (Female sphinxes appeared mainly in Greek mythology.) In fact, the largest and most famous of Egypt's stone sphinxes—the so-called Great Sphinx, which sits near the Pyramids at Giza— has a man's head. More specifically, it likely originally depicted Khafre, the fourth pharaoh of the Fourth Dynasty, whose enormous pyramid looms nearby. When it was carved in the mid-third millennium B.C., the sphinx was part of Khafre's funerary complex, which included temples, causeways, and statues, as well as the pyramid-tomb. The Great Sphinx—Egypt's largest statue—is roughly 66 feet (20m) tall and 240 feet (73m) long.

Similarly, most of ancient Egypt's numerous other carved sphinxes were associated with royalty or religion (or both) and were intended to blend with or enhance large-scale architectural settings. A renowned and stunning example consisted of the rows of ram-headed sphinxes that lined the sacred path leading from the Karnak temple complex to the Luxor temple,

The sacred path of ram-headed sphinxes that leads from the Karnak temple complex to the Luxor temple are a stunning example of Egyptian human-animal hybrid sculpture.

located a bit less than 2 miles (3km) to the south. Comparable lines of sphinxes were placed in front of other Egyptian temples, achieving a dramatic visual effect that awed the faithful.

Many people today who have never visited Egypt are familiar with such displays of sphinx statuary thanks to the late and legendary movie director Cecil B. DeMille. At great expense, for both his 1923 and 1956 versions of *The Ten Commandments*, his film artisans created a true-to-scale array of forty-two of these statues. (In a fascinating piece of trivia, after the 1923 version had finished shooting in a California desert, the sphinxes disappeared beneath the sand. Much later, in the 1980s, a group of American archaeologists hunted them down and partially excavated them.)

Immortalized in Stone

Although statues of gods and sphinxes were popular among the Egyptians, most of their largest colossi depicted human rulers, especially the pharaohs. This is perhaps not surprising. After all, the pharaohs sponsored the country's large-scale building projects. They were able to take advantage of that power and immortalize themselves in stone.

While some of Khafre's sculptors were creating the Great Sphinx at Giza, for example, others labored to carve several other huge statues of him. Some of these colossi stood silent guard both inside and outside of his mortuary temple. Similar hefty stone carvings of Khafre's Old Kingdom successor, Menkure, adorned the latter's funerary complex at Giza. Two

JULIUS CAESAR MEETS THE SPHINX

By Egypt's Greek and Roman periods, the Great Sphinx at Giza and other large Egyptian sphinxes had become objects of mystery and, because of their great age, symbols of longevity and eternal wisdom. In his 1900 play Caesar and Cleopatra, *Englishman George Bernard Shaw captured these qualities in the opening scene, in which the Roman general Julius Caesar approaches a sphinx in the moonlight and says:*

Hail, Sphinx. Salutation from Julius Caesar! I have wandered in many lands, seeking the lost regions from which my birth into this world exiled me. . . . In the little world yonder, Sphinx, my place is as high as yours in this great desert. Only I wander and you sit still. I conquer and you endure. I work and wonder, you watch and wait. I look up and am dazzled, look down and am darkened . . . whilst your eyes never turn from looking out—out of the world—to the lost region—the home from which we have strayed. Sphinx, you and I, strangers to the race of men, are no strangers to one another. . . . My way hither was the way of destiny; for I am he of whose genius you are the symbol: part brute, part woman, and part god—nothing of man in me at all. Have I read your riddle, Sphinx?

George Bernard Shaw. *Caesar and Cleopatra.* Baltimore: Penguin, 2006, pp. 25–26.

Four seventy-two-foot high, one-thousand-ton giant likenesses of Ramesses II sit in front of the temple at Abu Simbel in southern Egypt.

even larger stone colossi, each weighing between 11 and 13 tons (10 and 11.8t), were carved to depict the Middle Kingdom pharaoh Amenemhet III (reigned 1855–1808 B.C.).

Larger still were a number of giant statues carved during the New Kingdom. King Amenhotep III made two, each measuring some 50 feet (15m) in height and weighing 700 tons (635t). They show him sitting on his throne with his hands resting palms down on his knees. An earthquake later caused a crack in one of the statues that funneled the wind in an odd way, causing an eerie whistling sound. Over the centuries both locals and foreign visitors thought this sound might be the voice of a god. Some ancient Greek tourists suggested that the mythical character Memnon was singing to his mother, Eos, goddess of the dawn. Amenhotep's statues therefore became known as the Colossi of Memnon.

The biggest of all the ancient Egyptian colossi, besides the Great Sphinx, are the four giant likenesses of Ramesses II that sit in front of his great temple at Abu Simbel in southern Egypt. Each is 72 feet (22m) tall and weighs well in excess of 1,000 tons (907t). These truly awesome creations, among the

Of the few ancient Egyptian sculptors whose names have been preserved, two about whom at least a few facts are known are Bek and Thutmose. Both worked for the so-called maverick pharaoh, Akhenaton (born Amenhotep IV, reigned 1352–1336 B.C.). Evidence indicates that Bek was the son of Men, chief sculptor to Akhenaton's father, Amenhotep III. Bek supervised the creation of many of the statues of Akhenaton and his family erected in the pharaoh's new city, Akhetaton (which was later destroyed by Akhenaton's enemies). These sculptures employ the charming naturalistic style that this pharaoh preferred, one quite unique in Egyptian art. A surviving stone carving of Bek and his wife, Taheret, done by Bek himself, may be the earliest known self-portrait.

Bek's colleague, Thutmose, was the chief court sculptor during the later years of Akhenaton's reign. In 1912 German archaeologists excavating the ruins of Akhetaton found a work studio now thought to be Thutmose's. Also discovered there was Thutmose's masterpiece, a magnificent plaster bust of Akhenaton's wife, Nefertiti. This and other busts done of the pharaoh's family and courtiers by Thutmose have convinced modern-day scholars that he was one of the finest sculptors who ever lived.

Thutmose's magnificent bust of Queen Nefertiti was found in his newly excavated workshop in 1912.

world's greatest artistic treasures, were carved directly from an enormous cliff face. In the 1960s they, along with the whole temple, were threatened with submersion in a lake that was about to be created by a new dam. In an amazing feat, archaeologists and a large workforce carefully cut these priceless artifacts into individual blocks. Then they reassembled them perfectly on higher ground, where thousands of people continue to visit them each year.

Scenes Brought to Life

On a much smaller scale yet no less impressive than the colossi were the reliefs carved by Egyptian sculptors. Some tombs, temples, and palaces of the Old and Middle Kingdoms featured such carved scenes. But this type of sculpture reached its zenith during the New Kingdom.

Ramesses II is seen in his chariot vanquishing the Hittites at the battle of Kadesh in this relief from his temple at Abu Simbel.

Most relief sculptures appeared on walls on both the interiors and exteriors of structures and were neatly arranged into panels. The latter were usually divided into horizontal bands known as registers. A panel of reliefs could feature just one register or multiple ones, each arrayed above or below another. The registers were arranged in a chronological sequence to tell a story. The events in the lowest register on a wall were viewed as the most recent, for example. Meanwhile, within a *specific* register, the carvings lying nearest the biggest figure, almost always the king, were regarded as depicting the latest happenings. It was assumed that the actions of the figures further away had occurred prior to those key events.

Having determined the number of registers and which events they would depict, the sculptor and his assistants went to work. First, they applied to the wall a thick layer of smooth plaster. Next, some of the assistants did rough sketches of figures and objects on the dried plaster, usually in red paint. When these renderings were completed, the chief sculptor (or sculptors) made any necessary corrections in black paint. The final steps were the actual carving of the relief, using chisels, small hammers, and other tools, and painting the carvings in bright colors. Today those colors are gone, having been erased by centuries of erosion.

Among the most vivid and impressive surviving Egyptian wall reliefs are those carved by Ramesses II's artisans at Luxor, near Karnak. The subject of the registers is Ramesses's great victory over the Hittites (a people native to Anatolia, now Turkey) at Kadesh, in Syria. Military historian Mark Healy describes some of the dramatic scenes brought to life in this sculptural masterpiece. In one register, Ramesses

sits on his "golden throne" with his back to [his] camp. He is approached by a group of senior officers who break the news to him that the Hittite king and his army . . . are already camped in the vicinity of Kadesh. Above the officer group, Pharaoh's chariot and his horses . . . are readied for battle by his driver and shield-bearer. . . . In the register below this scene is shown the beating of the Hittite scouts [who have recently been] caught. [Another register shows] the Hittite chariots [as they] reach the camp and begin to assault it, [and] to the left of [Ramesses's] royal enclosure, Egyptian soldiers can be seen dragging Hittite crews from their chariots and dispatching [killing] them with their [curved] swords and bronze daggers.[36]

The Kadesh reliefs at Luxor and others like them have done more than aid modern-day scholars by describing key persons and events in Egyptian history. They, along with other surviving works by ancient Egypt's stone carvers, clearly show the tremendous artistry of these talented individuals. Two modern-day experts are far from alone in saying that they were among "the greatest sculptors the world has ever known."[37]

5

To Brighten People's Lives: Painting and Music

Today virtually everyone can agree that the world and life in general would be a lot duller without painting and music. The ancient Egyptians would have completely agreed with this judgment. Like people in nearly every age, they felt that painters and musicians brightened their lives in ways that most other artists could not. Another way that painters and musicians have traditionally been linked is the way each in a sense takes a different piece of art and translates it into his or her own artistic medium. The great nineteenth-century German composer Robert Schumann explained it well when he said that a painter gives a poem a visual dimension by turning it into a painting and a musician makes a picture come to life in music.

Similarly, ancient Egyptian painters and musicians routinely turned the sights and sounds of their world into artistic works that pleased the eye and soothed the ear. Practitioners of these two highly creative arts, amateurs and professionals alike, appear to have existed throughout Egyptian society. At least by the early years of the Old Kingdom, painters routinely decorated all manner of things, from the walls of houses, tombs, temples, and palaces; to statues, coffins, pottery, and baskets; to jewelry, furniture, and textiles. Meanwhile, musicians, among

Amateur and professional musicians composed music and entertained at dinner parties, weddings, victory celebrations, and funerals.

them the composers of the music, entertained at dinner parties, weddings, religious ceremonies, victory celebrations, and funerals. Existing depictions of Egyptian musicians suggest that vocalists often accompanied them. (In fact, some modern-day experts think that the musicians never formed strictly instrumental ensembles, but always provided background for singers.) Thus, both of these groups of artists regularly brightened the spirit of the human community in which they lived.

Very little is known about the lives, training, and social status of painters and musicians in ancient Egypt. However, some evidence has been found regarding how the work of painters was viewed by society's high and mighty. Paintings, which were very often large and detailed, were mandatory modes of decoration in royal tombs and palaces. The tombs of the nobility and other well-to-do people also contained handsome, sometimes exquisite paintings. In both life and death, therefore, the pharaohs, their relatives, and Egypt's rich and famous relied heavily on painters and their craft.

As a result, members of society's elite often rewarded painters for their contributions by giving them gifts. These typically consisted of cattle and other livestock, jewelry, slaves, and/or small plots of land. A handful of the best painters (along with the most skilled sculptors) also enjoyed the use of their own studios, which were built and maintained by members of the upper classes. In addition, on occasion a king took some painters (and/or sculptors) with him when he traveled, in case he might feel the need of their services. Nevertheless, like most other Egyptian artisans, even the finest painters almost always followed the custom of not signing their works, thereby remaining anonymous.

In comparison, the way that pharaohs, aristocrats, and other high-ranking individuals viewed musicians remains uncertain. Either singly or in groups, musicians did routinely entertain the powerful and well-to-do. It appears that music was also seen as a valuable asset to priests, temples, and religious functions. But so far, no evidence has been found indicating that musicians received any kind of special treatment by members of the upper classes.

Instruments and Ensembles

Still, there is ample evidence that Egyptians of all walks of life enjoyed music and listened to it on a regular basis. Depictions of people playing instruments, singing, and dancing appear frequently in surviving wall paintings and various forms of sculpture. These show that music was so pervasive in Egyptian life that it extended well beyond its use in entertainment and religious settings. Field-workers and construction laborers often sang while they worked, for instance. Indeed, "perhaps the best indication of the ancient Egyptians' sheer enjoyment of music," as well as their sense of humor, Egyptologist Ian Shaw points out, is a comic drawing dating from about 1200 B.C. It depicts an animal orchestra featuring "an ass with a large arched harp, a lion with a lyre [smaller harp], a crocodile with a lute [guitar-like instrument], and a monkey with a double oboe."[38]

Of the instruments in that charming cartoon, the double oboe was among several wind instruments used in ancient Egypt. Others common ones included the flute, initially made of

In this wall painting from the tomb of Thutmose III's vizier Rekhmere, a woman is seen playing the harp. This early stringed instrument may have been borrowed from Mesopotamia.

reeds or pieces of hollowed-out wood, and later metal; a clarinet-like instrument similar to the modern Egyptian *zummara*; the double-flute, or *aulos*, introduced to Egypt by the Greeks in the 200s B.C.; the trumpet, first used to sound the attack or retreat in battle; and animal horns of assorted sizes, some of them resembling the ancient Hebrew *shofar* (made from a ram's horn).

The Egyptians had string instruments, too. Possibly the earliest was a harp with eleven or more strings, which they likely borrowed from Mesopotamia. Others included the seven-stringed lyre and the lute. About the latter, one expert says it was similar to "a mandolin with a long, oval resonating [vibrating] body [made] out of wood covered partly in leather [and] partly by a thin sheet of wood with an opening to release the sound."[39]

In addition, there were percussion instruments, which kept the beat and added exotic color to the music. Among them was the *sistrum*, a kind of hand rattle with small, cymbal-like metal strips attached. Others included ivory clappers that the player slapped against her or his hand or body, and various-size drums that a player hit with either a stick or the hand.

Sometimes one or two percussionists accompanied a single harp, flute, or lute. But as remains the case today, there were all sorts of combinations of instruments that ranged all the way up to a full orchestra. Modern-day musicians have reproduced these instruments and played them in such ensembles. Regrettably, however, there is no way to know what the original melodies, harmonies, and rhythms were like because, so far as is known, the Egyptians never developed a practical kind of musical notation (written notes). As an educated guess, scholar Eugen Strouhal suggests that the sounds lay "somewhere between those of modern Arab music and those of Black Africa."[40]

From Hymns to Love Songs

One aspect of ancient Egyptian music that *has* survived consists of the lyrics, or words, of a number of the songs sung by the vocalists who accompanied the musicians. A number of these songs were hymns meant to honor the gods, which is not surprising considering how devoutly religious the Egyptians were. Perhaps the most famous example was composed by the New Kingdom pharaoh Akhenaton. He introduced a new deity—

AN ANCIENT HYMN SET TO MODERN MUSIC

t is unknown whether the words of Akhenaton's hymn to Aten were originally chanted or sung, or whether the hymn was performed by solo voice or choir. More than three thousand years later, the maverick pharaoh's beautiful tribute to his god was revived in a splendid manner as part of the musical score for Twentieth Century Fox's lavish 1954 film *The Egyptian*. The plot revolves around an Egyptian doctor who becomes court physician and friend to Akhenaton. In one of the film's climactic sequences, the pharaoh's followers are seen worshipping Aten, with the great hymn echoing around them. The music, scored for a large choir and full orchestra, was composed by legendary Hollywood composer Alfred Newman, winner of numerous Academy Awards. The marriage of Newman's music and Akhenaton's written words creates what noted film music critic Jack Smith calls an "exotic, mystical quality." It is "wonderfully ethereal [heavenly]," he adds, "a profound expression of blissful, devoted worship." (The full score for *The Egyptian*, including Akhenaton's hymn, resurrected in glory from ancient obscurity, was rerecorded and remastered in 2000.)

Quoted in *The Egyptian*. Marco Polo, 2000, booklet accompanying compact disc, p. 11.

Aten, whose face, this eccentric king believed, was the sun's blinding disk. His long hymn to that god reads in part:

> You shine beautiful on the horizon of heaven,
> O Living Disk, who did live from the beginning.
> When you rise in the eastern horizon,
> You fill every land with your beauty.
> Your rays embrace the lands even to the limit

Of all you have created. . . .
You reach into every land, uniting all
For your beloved son, Akhenaten![41]

Akhenaton's attempted religious revolution, in which he tried to replace the traditional Egyptian gods with Aten, failed. Following the so-called maverick pharaoh's death, those other

In this tomb relief two women are depicted playing the harp and singing. Song was an important aspect of Egyptian cultural life.

deities were restored, including the New Kingdom's all-powerful creator god, Amun-Ra.

The Egyptians sang all manner of other songs. Some were recited by gangs of laborers as they transported heavy stone blocks from quarries to waiting worksites. Others honored the pharaohs, including victory odes that musicians and singers performed for the kings and their troops on their return from foreign wars. Still other songs were composed by or for people in love.

Painters' Tools and Conventions

The primary tools that Egyptian songwriters used to create these poignant passages were words. In a like manner, Egyptian painters had their own principal tools—in this case their paints, consisting of pigments taken from common natural materials. Red, yellow, and brown, for example, came from widely available minerals, including iron oxide. They made blue paint by mixing a form of copper ore, sand, and a mineral salt known as natron and heating them. Green, of course, came from combining the blue and yellow pigments, and orange from mixing the red and yellow ones. Finally, black was made from soot and white from the minerals chalk and gypsum. Whatever pigments were used, the artisans mixed them with water and a glue derived from the acacia tree. The palettes that held these pigments were usually homemade and consisted of pieces of pottery or wood that had been cut and shaped according to the preference of the individual artist.

As is still true today, the other tools essential to the ancient Egyptian painters' craft were brushes. In most cases they were fashioned from the stems of marsh reeds, countless acres of which grew along the banks of the Nile. Typically, a painter chewed on the end of a reed to fray it and thereby create what today would be called the bristles of the brush.

Having assembled his paints and brushes, the artist got to work. Modern-day painters most often employ whatever styles

A REMARKABLE LACK OF CHANGE

Researcher Dianne Durante here describes the curious tendency among ancient Egyptian painters and other artists to employ the same static style used in prior Egyptian art. She also mentions the one major exception—the more realistic style used by the pharaoh Akhenaton's artists.

Over the course of 3000 years, the most remarkable feature of Egyptian art is the lack of change. It is easy to recognize the differences between a Greek sculpture from 600 B.C. and one from 400 B.C., or a French painting from 1400 A.D. and one from 1600 A.D. While the Egyptians did learn very early how to represent standing or sitting human beings reasonably well, they did not study the movements of bones and muscles beneath the skin, nor attempt to represent figures relaxing, moving violently, or expressing strong feelings. No matter what the figure is doing, the muscles do not change shape. Little effort is made to show any individual characteristics. The only notable exception in the Egyptian style comes during the reign of the New Kingdom Pharaoh Akhenaten. He preferred artists to render him and his wife, Nefertiti, as realistically as they could. The work of this period features an emotional intensity not found at any other time in ancient Egyptian art.

Dianne Durante. "Egyptian Painting." Beyond Books.com. www.beyondbooks.com/art11/2b.asp.

This painted limestone relief from el-Amarna depicts Akhenaton and Nefertiti making offerings to the sun god Aton. Akhenaton preferred that his artisans depict him and his wife as realistically as possible.

This ancient palette of the painter Dedia shows paint wells and four small brushes. Traces of red paint can still be seen.

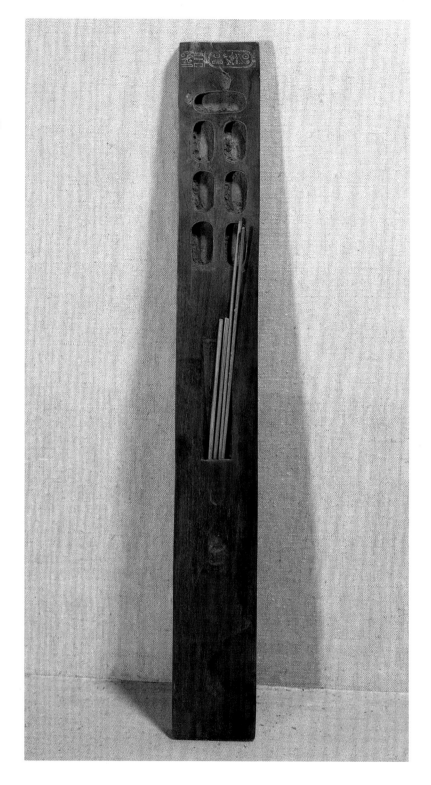

and techniques that most satisfy them and end up making their own individual artistic statements. In contrast, and with extremely few exceptions, Egyptian painters followed a series of conventions (accepted rules and methods) that had been handed down from prior generations and rarely changed.

For instance, some conventions called for using certain colors to symbolize, or stand for, specific objects or facets of life or nature. The painter applied bright red pigment to signify blood or evil and white paint to denote happiness or new beginnings. Similarly, brownish-red was always used for men's skin; pale yellow for women's skin; green for water and themes related to youth; blue for the sky and the hair of any gods portrayed; and black for rich soil and certain themes dealing with death and the afterlife.

Other accepted painting conventions involved the way figures and objects were arranged on the wall (or other surface to be painted). As was the case for sculptors creating reliefs, painters frequently lined up their subjects in registers, one above another. One reason that registers evolved was that the artists did not attempt to show people and objects in a realistic, three-dimensional manner. They were perfectly capable of doing so. Instead they chose to follow strict customs and work in two dimensions while employing specific, artificial conventions to convey the idea of depth. For instance, depth and the notion of increasing distance were routinely implied by making one image slightly overlap another. "When items overlap," noted scholar Gay Robins explains, "what is behind is further from the viewer than what is in front. [Also] when items are stacked above one another in a register, those higher up are behind those lower down."[42]

More familiar to people today is the so-called Egyptian pose. In it, Robins says, "the rendering of the human figure forms a composite built up from its individual parts. Thus, the head is usually shown in profile with a full-view eyebrow and eye set into it. The shoulders [and chest] of formal figures are most frequently depicted full view, but the waist, buttocks, and limbs are in profile."[43] In this way, another expert points out, one human figure is "seen from several different angles, blended into a single form. This was intended to combine the most lifelike aspects of each area of the body."[44]

Five Thousand Years and Counting

These and other conventions for a planned painting could be worked out in preliminary sketches, done by the chief painter on a plaster-coated wooden board or a piece of broken pottery. Then one or more lower-level artists, called *sesh kedut*, did full-scale rough outlines on the walls to be painted. Grids helped the artists maintain proper proportions during the sketching phase. By the early years of the Middle Kingdom, a typical grid had eighteen squares, which increased to twenty-one squares several centuries later. "The Egyptians could lay out these [grid]lines on any surface," art historian Rita Freed writes, "to reproduce identically-proportioned figures of whatever size they wanted."[45]

The grid lines were typically red. The present prevailing theory is that a painter lightly coated a cord with red paint, pulled it taut in front of a wall or other surface, then snapped it, creating a line. (A few experts think the artists used a straight-edged wooden ruler and painted the line against it with a thin brush.) Usually, an artist followed tradition, which dictated a fixed ratio of squares to body parts. He knew that the hairline of the painted figure should appear in a certain square within the grid, for instance. Similarly, the lower neck, elbow, knee, and other body parts routinely appeared in specific grid squares. In this way, no matter how big or small the surface and grid, the figure represented had more or less the same proportions.

After the sketches had been applied to the grid, another group of painters, known simply as *sesh*, began applying the paint, carefully staying within the lines of the sketches. This could be particularly difficult when the wall paintings were inside tombs. (It was thought that tomb paintings of gods, people, food, tools, and other objects would come to life after the tomb was sealed and become usable by the deceased person in the afterlife.) Owing to the lack of natural light in such crypts, painters used oil-burning stone or pottery lamps, candles, and/or torches to illuminate their work.

Although ancient Egyptian painters labored in all kinds of settings and decorated numerous surfaces and objects, tomb paintings turned out to be their most important legacy. This is because the thick layers of rock surrounding the chambers protected these works from weathering and other causes of erosion

Egyptian tomb painters first painted a grid of squares and used a fixed ratio of squares to body parts to produce identically proportioned figures of whatever size they desired.

for long time periods. Some therefore still retain some of their original luster, preserving the legacy of otherwise forgotten artists who toiled to help their compatriots attain and enjoy eternal life. In the fitting words of art expert Dianne Durante: "Egyptian painting astounds [us] in part because it's lasted for almost 5,000 years and counting. More incredible is that Egyptian art—in all its detail—deals with the major questions that artists have wrestled with throughout time. Life, afterlife, religion, and the natural world are not just Egyptian concerns. They are eternal human concerns."[46]

"A Remarkable Legacy": Egypt's Superb Craftsmen

The Egyptians did not have a word for *artist* in the modern sense. To them all artists and artisans, no matter what their specialty, were craftsmen. So a regrettable difficulty arises when writing about these individuals, one having to do with language and culture. In a number of other cultures, including those of ancient Greece and Rome and the modern West, the term *craftsman* conjures up a picture of a skilled worker. By comparison, the word *artist* indicates someone who works from his or her imagination and inspiration and is thereby quite different from a craftsman.

This was not the case in ancient Egypt, however, where the line between craftsman and artist blurred. Thus, calling woodworkers, metalsmiths, jewelers, and other skilled Egyptians "craftsmen" should not be interpreted to mean that they were any less talented than that culture's architects, sculptors, and painters. The late British Egyptologist T.G.H. James pointed out that the many finely made surviving artifacts from ancient Egypt are all of equal artistic value, no matter what modern categories and labels one assigns them. Skill, he said,

> combined with a true feeling for the craft concerned, and a sympathy with the materials employed in the craft,

These superbly crafted ebony and ivory game boards were found in the tomb of Tutankhamun and, along with other discovered artifacts, attest to the excellence of Egyptian arts and crafts.

were all necessary for the making of well-designed, finely decorated, and superbly finished objects of the kinds which have survived in surprising quantities. . . . [The Egyptians] left a remarkable legacy of what are now, unfortunately, called "the minor arts." . . . The contents of the tomb of Tutankhamun [King Tut] in themselves form the ultimate testimony of [the overall] achievement [of Egyptian arts and crafts that] have been amply exemplified by the many choice pieces preserved in [both museum and private] collections throughout the world.[47]

Another important difference between ancient Egyptian and modern craft specialists relates to the nature of their employment. The vast majority of modern-day craftsmen are independent contractors who work for themselves and are hired to do specific jobs. In Egypt, in contrast, most craftsmen labored full-time in workshops owned by the royal palace, temples, provincial governors, wealthy households, and so forth. It was not unusual to see workshops for furniture makers, jewelers, and other specialists adjoining one another, and in some cases these and other artisans coexisted in a single workshop.

Working with Metals

One exception to this common grouping of craft specialties in the same area may have been the workshop of the metalsmith, or more simply, smith. The combination of the smoke from his furnace, the odors of the heated metals he worked with, and his own sweat must have given his shop a distinctive, if not downright unpleasant, smell. A passage from the famous Middle Kingdom document known as the *Satire of Trades* reads, "I have seen the smith at work at the opening of his furnace. With fingers like claws of a crocodile [i.e., scaly], he stinks more than fish [eggs]."[48]

Egyptian smiths, or *bedjty* (named for their popular metal vases), initially worked with copper, the earliest metal used in Egypt. Over time, they became adept in smelting and casting bronze (an alloy of copper and tin), lead, gold, silver, electrum (an alloy of gold and silver), and brass (an alloy of copper and zinc). None of these substances were abundant in the country. Although Egypt did have some mines, most metal ores (rocks containing veins of metal) were imported from foreign regions.

Whether mined locally or imported, the ore first underwent smelting, the process of separating the metal from the rock in which it was encased. The smith did this by putting chunks of ore in a stone container and heating it over an open fire. Because a normal fire was not hot enough, during the Old and New Kingdoms, the smith increased its temperature by blowing air into it through hollow reeds. A major advance that

This reconstruction of a painting found in Thebes shows artisans at work on various crafts. The two men at lower left are using the older method of stoking the fire by blowing air through hollow reeds. This approach was replaced by the bellows during the New Kingdom.

occurred during the New Kingdom was the introduction of a simple type of bellows. It consisted of a leather-covered pottery container with a protruding tube. The smith used his open palm or his foot to press down on the air-filled leather, forcing the air out through the tube and into the fire. It became customary for him or an assistant to employ two bellows at once, alternately pushing on them with hands or feet.

Having separated out the copper or other metal, which was now hot and very soft, the smith cast, bent, cut, or otherwise manipulated it into the desired shape. One common method was to pour the metal into a shallow stone dish and allow it to cool and harden a bit. Then the smith used a stone hammer to beat the still-hot lump of metal into shape.

Among a few more advanced metal-casting methods that eventually came into use is one often called hollow casting. The first step was to fashion a wooden model of the desired object, surround it with clay, and bake it in an oven. When the clay had hardened, the smith removed the wooden core, creating a hollow earthenware mold. The last steps were to pour heated, softened metal into the mold, wait for the metal to cool and solidify, and then break off the earthenware, leaving behind the metal artifact.

Copper and bronze objects made using this and other hollow-casting techniques were usually solid. However, gold and silver were generally handled differently because they were more scarce and valuable. A few gold objects—like the masks and coffins made for the burial chambers of the pharaohs—were solid. But most gold was beaten into extremely thin sheets, called gold leaf, and added to objects made of wood, bronze, or some other material, a process called gilding. (Silver was often beaten into leaf form, too.) One of the most striking surviving artifacts made this way is a gilded wooden statue of the minor goddess Nephthys (sister of Osiris, god of the afterlife) found in the pharaoh Tutankhamun's tomb in the 1920s.

Jewelry Materials and Forms

One of the chief uses for gold and silver leaf was making fine jewelry. The Egyptians made exquisite jewelry throughout ancient times (although modern-day experts contend that the highest-quality items were produced during the Middle Kingdom). In addition to covering wood, copper, or bronze with gold or silver leaf, the jewelers used a wide array of materials. These included solid gold, silver, or electrum; plain copper, bronze, or brass; ivory; glass; polished colored pebbles; seashells; various semiprecious stones (like carnelian, turquoise, lapis lazuli, rock crystal, calcite, jasper, garnet, and feldspar); and faience (a shiny coating made from crushed quartz).

These and other substances were made into a number of forms of jewelry worn by both women and men of all ages. (Also, fine jewelry was used to ornament both statues of the gods and the dead bodies of members of the upper classes, who could afford such expensive items.) One of the most common forms, then as now, was the necklace. The simplest kind had a single strand of stones, metal beads, glass, or shells. Thicker, more elaborate ones, called *wesekh*, were popular among the rich and famous, as were pectorals. A typical pectoral featured a small, highly ornamented plaque that hung down from the necklace strands. Inside the plaque was a carved and painted miniature scene. A magnificent surviving example is a pectoral plaque given by the Middle Kingdom pharaoh Senusret II to his daughter. Now on display in New York's Metropolitan Museum of Art, it features two falcons flanking a human figure and a scarab beetle, all made from inlays of gold, turquoise, garnet, and other semiprecious stones.

Among the other common kinds of ancient Egyptian jewelry were bracelets, anklets, armlets, rings, earrings, fillets (decorative bands worn in the hair), and amulets. The latter were believed to have magical powers that protected the wearer. Amulets were created from diverse materials, including copper, bronze, iron, gold, silver, semiprecious stones, wood, and bone. One of the more common shapes was the life sign, the ankh, consisting of a cross with a small oval loop at the top. Also popular were amulets shaped like scarab beetles and those bearing the *udjat*, the sacred and stylish symbol of the eye of the savior god Horus.

Egypt's Splendid Stone Vessels

Jewelry remained one of the most beautiful expressions of Egyptian arts and crafts throughout pharaonic times. That was the period in which the pharaohs ruled, lasting from about 3100 to 30 B.C. In stark contrast was the lesser quality of the work of most potters during that era. A majority of pottery, or ceramics, which was called "coarse ware" and used by most Egyptians, was made from Nile mud and of fairly basic and unremarkable quality. Therefore, it cannot be classified as fine art. Its makers were the individuals whom the author of the *Satire of Trades* had in mind when he scorned the potter as one who "grubs in the mud more than a pig in order to fire his pots."[49]

There were two exceptions to this general rule of unexceptional pottery. Well before pharaonic times, in the period from about 5500 to 4000 B.C., Egyptian ceramics were of much

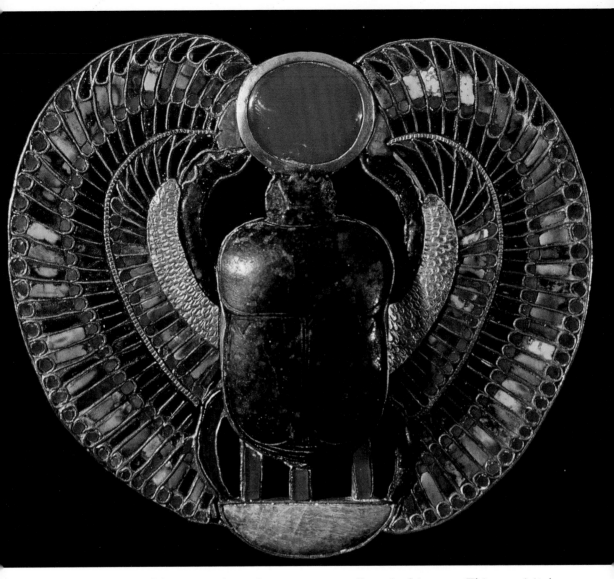

higher quality. The second exception was a small-scale faience industry in which dinnerware, vases, figurines, and other items were made from stone dust during pharaonic times. However, although the faience products were higher in quality than ordinary pottery, they were expensive and therefore used almost exclusively by members of the upper classes.

Some Egyptian artisans in a sense made up for the baseness of coarse ware. They did this by creating most of the same items potters did—cups, bowls, vases, storage containers, and

This exquisitely crafted pectoral found in Tutankhamun's tomb is made of gold, lapis lazuli, and turquoise.

Among the more popular craft items in Egypt's great city of Alexandria in Ptolemaic times (the last three centuries B.C.) were fine vases, lamps, bowls, and figurines made of faience. This glaze, most often colored apple-green, was not new to that era. Indeed, by that time faience, made from crushed quartz, had been made in Egypt for almost three thousand years. The somewhat iridescent, or gleaming, surfaces of faience objects made them both more beautiful and more expensive than the rather dull coarse pottery used by poor Egyptians.

To make faience, artisans first crushed hunks of quartz by pounding them with stone balls or hammers. Then they mixed the powder they had produced with water and small quantities of lime or plant ash. The result was a paste that could be shaped into a wide range of items, including amulets, decorative tiles, beads, vases, cups, plates, figurines, and dozens of others. After forming the desired item, the artisan applied the glaze, also in the form of a paste. Most faience glazes were green or blue, derived from copper compounds, although other colors, such as red, yellow, and black, were used from time to time. Finally, the object was fired in a kiln to harden it. Sometimes the artisan also painted designs of various kinds on the object to further add to its attractiveness.

This lotus-shaped cup from the thirteenth century B.C. is an example of faience glaze. To make it, artisans crushed quartz and mixed it with water and lime or plant ash.

so forth—using a method that *can* be classified as artistic. It is often called the art of making stone vessels. A majority of these splendid pieces utilized softer types of stone, including sandstone, limestone, and alabaster. The first step was to craft the contours of the vessel's outer surfaces. The artisan did this by pounding them with a handheld pick or stone ball, both made of a harder stone such as dolerite. Polishing the outer surfaces was done with a piece of sandstone.

Hollowing out the vessel's interior was more difficult and time-consuming. The most common approach was to employ an abrasive like quartz sand. When rubbed vigorously on the stone surface, it could grind down even a substance of the same hardness, as diamond dust is used to cut diamonds. Thus, the late historian Lionel Casson explained, "vases that were cylindrical could be scooped out by endless drilling, with the [drill] bit turned in wetted fine quartz sand, the sand doing the actual cutting. The craftsmen's skill was so accomplished that they were able to leave the walls of a vase paper-thin, no more than a millimeter in thickness."[50]

Borrowed Glassmaking Methods

No less skilled than these stone vessel makers were Egypt's glassmakers. As late as the final century of the Middle Kingdom (the 1600s B.C.), glass items in Egypt mainly took the form of small beads and other minor jewelry elements. It was not until the early years of the New Kingdom that an industry able to produce glass vases and other vessels took root in the country. It appears that this happened as a result of some Egyptian military expeditions into Syria, where glassmaking techniques were well established. Impressed, the pharaohs who organized these forays brought those techniques back and set up workshops. At first these were near the royal palace, so that the government could tightly control the industry. As a result, locally made glass vessels long remained expensive and were used mainly by members of the upper classes.

Several methods were employed for making glass in Egypt. In the most basic one, called core forming, the artisan melted sand until it became essentially liquid glass. Then he took an ordinary pottery cup or other piece of coarse ware and dipped it into the molten glass, causing a layer of the hot liquid to build up on it. When the glass layer had cooled and hardened, the artisan used a thin, pointed rod to break up and extract the pottery core. That left behind a glass shell that resembled the original cup or other pottery item.

For a number of political, economic, and logistical reasons, Egypt's glassmaking industry declined in the later years of the New Kingdom and had disappeared by about 1050 B.C. However, more than seven centuries later, in the early years of the Ptolemaic dynasty (the late 300s B.C.), glassmaking revived in Egypt. During an era of economic boom, Ptolemaic Egyptian merchants and artisans once again looked to Syria, which was still a major source of glass. New workshops were built in Alexandria, in the Nile Delta, and soon Egypt made as many glass products as Syria did. Because the age-old methods remained in use, these products were still quite expensive and out of the reach of most Egyptians.

Fortunately for those average Egyptians, this situation changed not long after the close of the Ptolemaic era. During the first century B.C., the art of glassmaking underwent a true revolution when some Syrian artisans (whose identities are unknown) invented glassblowing. As scholar Eugen Strouhal says, "The new discovery increased production many-fold and glass then ceased to be either a rarity or an upper-class prerogative [privilege]." Nevertheless, the best glassware remained of extremely high quality. "It was a highly artistic craft," Strouhal writes, "and gifted individuals had a chance to become acknowledged masters."[51]

Creators for Eternity

Unlike glassmaking, which first became a viable industry fairly late in Egyptian history, the craft of woodworking, or carpentry, developed at least four to five centuries before the start of

A blue glass bottle from the Amarna period, fourteenth century, B.C. The Egyptians borrowed glassmaking techniques from the Syrians, and the pharaohs made it a tightly controlled government industry.

THEY WELCOMED DEATH

Much of the copper the Egyptians used came from mines in the country's eastern deserts, the Sinai Peninsula, and Nubia, lying directly south of Egypt. Gold came from a number of regions, including the deserts of what is now Sudan. Most of the workers in these mines were slaves, either war captives or convicted criminals, often accompanied by their families. In the second century B.C., a Greek geographer named Agatharchides described the plight of the workers in a gold mine in Sudan:

They do their quarrying with [small oil] lamps bound to their foreheads, following the white gleam like a vein [of gold]. Constantly shifting the position of their bodies, they knock down chunks—not according to their bodily condition and strength, but to the foreman's eye, who never fails to administer punishment with the whip. Young boys, creeping through the galleries hacked out by the miners, laboriously collect what has fallen down on the gallery floor and carry it outside the entrance. From them the rock is taken over by the more elderly and many of the feeble, who . . . pound the rock vigorously with iron pestles until they have made the biggest piece the size of a pea. . . . All who suffer the fate just described feel that death is more desirable than life.

Quoted in Lionel Casson. *Everyday Life in Ancient Egypt.* Baltimore: Johns Hopkins University Press, 2001, p. 77.

the Old Kingdom. Carpenters learned to use both native woods and foreign imports. The leading local varieties were date palm, tamarisk, acacia, and willow, while the imported ones included cypress, elm, cedar, juniper, oak, and pine.

To work these materials, the carpenters initially used copper saws, drills, borers, hand axes, awls, and chisels. Over time, however, bronze and, later, iron versions of these tools were added to the standard woodworking tool kit. Ancient Egyptian metal saws deserve special mention because the cutting edges of their teeth pointed toward the handle. This made them "pull" saws, as opposed to most modern versions, which are "push" saws with the teeth pointing away from the handle.

Utilizing the diverse wood types and excellent tools at their disposal, Egyptian carpenters created objects, particularly furniture, chests, and chariots, of extremely high quality. Attesting to this are the throne, tall bureau, dozens of storage chests, six beds, and six full-sized chariots found by Howard Carter in King Tut's tomb. All are of superb workmanship.

Moreover, Egypt's woodworkers were not chance flukes among that country's artisans. Rather, they made up only a few drops in an immense pool of talent that can stand beside the artistic community of any nation in history. That says a lot when one considers how long ago Egyptian civilization reached its zenith and how many imposing and impressive cultures followed it. As he so often did when capturing the essences of past peoples, Casson nailed it when he said that the greatness of ancient Egyptian art "lies not in the quality and durability of the art itself: the massive symmetry of the pyramids, the sophistication of the sculpture, and the charm of the paintings and reliefs. The Egyptians created for eternity, and nothing that humans have fashioned [since has] proved more lasting than their great works of art."[52]

Notes

Introduction: "No Word for Art"

1. Howard Carter. *The Tomb of Tut-ankhamun*. 1923. Reprint, London: Dover, 1985, pp. 95–96.
2. Lionel Casson. *Ancient Egypt*. New York: Time-Life, 1983, p. 117.
3. Casson. *Ancient Egypt*, p. 13.
4. Rita M. Freed. "Egyptian Art." In *Ancient Egypt*, edited by David P. Silverman. New York: Oxford University Press, 2003, p. 212.

Chapter 1: Monument Builders: The Crews, Tools, and Methods

5. Peter Der Manuelian. "Tombs and Temples." In *Ancient Egypt*, edited by David P. Silverman. New York: Oxford University Press, 2003, p. 208.
6. Rosalie David. *Handbook to Life in Ancient Egypt*. New York: Facts On File, 2003, pp. 166–167.
7. David. *Handbook to Life in Ancient Egypt*, p. 167.
8. Dieter Arnold. *Building in Egypt: Pharaonic Stone Masonry*. Oxford: Oxford University Press, 1997, p. 4.
9. Herodotus. *The Histories*. Translated by Aubrey de Sélincourt. New York: Penguin, 2003, pp. 178–179.

10. Quoted in Jill Kamil. *The Ancient Egyptians: Life in the Old Kingdom*. Cairo: American University in Cairo Press, 1997, pp. 76–77.
11. Kamil. *The Ancient Egyptians*, p. 77.
12. I.E.S. Edwards. *The Pyramids of Egypt*. New York: Penguin, 1993, pp. 211–212.
13. Zahi Hawass. "The Discovery of the Tombs of the Pyramid Builders." Guardian's Egypt. http://www.guardians.net/hawass/ buildtomb.htm.
14. Hawass. "The Discovery of the Tombs of the Pyramid Builders."
15. Eugen Strouhal. *Life of the Ancient Egyptians*. Norman: University of Oklahoma Press, 1992, p. 175.

Chapter 2: Wonders of the World: The Great Pyramids

16. Quoted in Desmond Stewart. *The Pyramids and the Sphinx*. New York: Newsweek Book Division, 1979, p. 140.
17. Quoted in Peter Clayton and Martin Price. *The Seven Wonders of the Ancient World*. New York: Barnes and Noble, 1993, p. 31.
18. Pliny the Elder. *Natural History: A*

Selection. Translated by John F. Healy. New York: Penguin, 1991, p. 352.

19. Stewart. *The Pyramids and the Sphinx*, pp. 35–36.

20. Quoted in Josephine Mayer and Tom Prideaux, eds. *Never to Die: The Egyptians in Their Own Words.* New York: Viking, 1938, pp. 42–44.

21. Herodotus. *The Histories*, p. 179.

22. Kevin Jackson and Jonathan Stamp. *Building the Great Pyramid.* Toronto: Firefly, 2003, p. 72.

Chapter 3: Palaces to Pylons: Egypt's Monumental Arts

23. Lionel Casson. *Everyday Life in Ancient Egypt.* Baltimore: Johns Hopkins University Press, 2001, p. 66.

24. David. *Handbook to Life in Ancient Egypt*, p. 182.

25. Herodotus. *The Histories*, p. 143.

26. Ian Shaw and Paul Nicholson. *The Dictionary of Ancient Egypt.* New York: Harry N. Abrams, 2003, p. 285.

27. Steven Snape. *Egyptian Temples.* Buckinghamshire, UK: Shire, 1999, p. 33.

28. Ian Shaw. *Egyptian Warfare and Weapons.* Buckinghamshire, UK: Shire, 1999, p. 15.

29. Shaw. *Egyptian Warfare and Weapons*, p. 22.

30. Quoted in Pliny the Elder. *Natural History*, p. 353.

Chapter 4: Statues and Reliefs: The Art of Stone Sculpture

31. Percy Bysshe Shelley. *Miscellaneous and Posthumous Poems of Percy Bysshe Shelley.* London: W. Benbow, 1826, p. 100.

32. Gay Robins. *Egyptian Statues.* Buckinghamshire, UK: Shire, 2003, p. 7.

33. David. *Handbook to Life in Ancient Egypt*, p. 307.

34. Robins. *Egyptian Statues*, p. 9.

35. Casson. *Everyday Life in Ancient Egypt*, p. 73.

36. Mark Healy. *The Warrior Pharaoh: Rameses II and the Battle of Qadesh.* Oxford: Osprey, 2000, p. 65.

37. Mayer and Prideaux. *Never to Die*, p. 65.

Chapter 5: To Brighten People's Lives: Painting and Music

38. Shaw and Nicholson. *The Dictionary of Ancient Egypt*, p. 192.

39. Strouhal. *Life of the Ancient Egyptians*, p. 44.

40. Strouhal. *Life of the Ancient Egyptians*, p. 45.

41. Quoted in Mayer and Prideaux. *Never to Die*, p. 162.

42. Gay Robins. *The Art of Ancient Egypt.* Cambridge, MA: Harvard University Press, 2008, p. 21.

43. Robins. *The Art of Ancient Egypt*, p. 21.

44. Strouhal. *Life of the Ancient Egyptians*, p. 163.

45. Freed. "Egyptian Art," p. 217.

46. Dianne Durante. "Egyptian Painting." Beyond Books.com. www.beyondbooks.com/art11/2b.asp.

Chapter 6: "A Remarkable Legacy": Egypt's Superb Craftsmen

47. T.G.H. James. *Pharaoh's People: Scenes from Life in Imperial Egypt.* New York: Tauris Parke, 2003, pp. 182–183.

48. Quoted in Miriam Lichtheim. *Ancient Egyptian Literature.* Vol. 1. *The Old and Middle Kingdoms.* Berkeley and Los Angeles: University of California Press, 2006, p. 186.

49. Quoted in Lichtheim. *Ancient Egyptian Literature*, p. 186.

50. Casson. *Everyday Life in Ancient Egypt*, p. 69.

51 Strouhal. *Life of the Ancient Egyptians*, p. 144.

52. Casson. *Ancient Egypt*, p. 128.

akhet: An Egyptian hieroglyph (picture sign) symbolizing the horizon.

alloy: A mixture of two or more metals.

amulet: An object, either worn or carried, thought to have magical properties that would protect the owner.

ankh: The Egyptian symbol of life, or an object shaped like it.

aulos: A double flute imported into Egypt from Greece.

bedjty: Metalsmiths.

benben: In Egyptian mythology, the primeval (very ancient) mound of creation and first dry land in the world; or a sacred stone representation of the mound.

brass: A mixture of copper and zinc.

bronze: A mixture of copper and tin.

casing stones: The smooth limestone blocks forming the outside surfaces of pyramids and some other structures.

coarse ware: Simple, inexpensive pottery made from local Egyptian silt and clay.

colossi: Giant statues.

corvée labor: In past ages, citizens who worked on government projects to fulfill tax or other obligations.

crenellation: The notched effect in the battlements of forts, castles, and other ancient and medieval structures.

cult temple: A temple used primarily for standard worship of a god or gods.

dolerite: A very hard type of stone often used by the ancient Egyptians to make tools.

dynasty: A line of rulers belonging to a single family.

Egyptology: The branch of archaeology dealing specifically with ancient Egypt.

electrum: A mixture of gold and silver.

faience: A glistening substance made from crushed quartz that the Egyptians used widely in the production of pottery and jewelry.

gilding: The process of covering an object with a thin layer of gold.

hypostyle hall: A large interior chamber whose roof is held up by numerous columns evenly distributed across the room.

kedu: Potters or mud brick makers in ancient Egypt.

lute: A guitarlike instrument.

lyre: A small harp.

mastaba: A low, rectangular tomb made of mud bricks or stone.

monumental: Large-scale; a term usually used to describe large buildings.

mortuary temple: A temple built mainly to maintain a deceased pharaoh's spirit and ensure its continued connection to the gods.

necropolis: A burial ground.

obelisk: A tall, narrow, pointed stone spire that stood near the gate of an Egyptian temple.

pectoral: A large, highly ornamented necklace worn by the well-to-do in ancient Egypt.

pylon: A large, flat-topped ceremonial gateway that became a common feature of Egyptian temples, particularly in the New Kingdom.

register: A horizontal band of paintings or sculptures on a wall, vase, or some other surface.

relief (or bas-relief): A carving raised partly into three dimensions from a flat surface.

scarab: An amulet or some other object in the shape of a scarab beetle.

scribe: A literate person who wrote letters and kept written records for a living.

sesh: Painters who filled in the outlines created by sketch artists, or assistant painters known as *sesh kedut*.

sistrum: A native Egyptian musical instrument consisting of a handheld rattle with small cymbal-like metal disks attached.

sledge: A sledlike device on which ancient workers carried large stones and statues.

sphinx: In ancient Egypt, a mythical creature combining the features or traits of a human and an animal, most often a lion; or a statue representing such a creature.

udjat: An amulet or other object that portrayed the Eye of Horus, a religious symbol thought to have magical properties.

vizier: The chief administrator to the pharaoh.

wesekh: A broad band of beads or other decorations worn like a necklace.

zaa: A group of two hundred Egyptian construction workers.

For More Information

Books

Carol Andrews. *Ancient Egyptian Jewelry*. London: British Museum, 1997. A well-written, informative introduction to the subject.

Dieter Arnold. *Building in Egypt: Pharaonic Stone Masonry*. Oxford: Oxford University Press, 1997. A thorough, well-illustrated, scholarly overview of Egyptian building methods.

Lionel Casson. *Everyday Life in Ancient Egypt*. Baltimore: Johns Hopkins University Press, 2001. An accessible examination of ancient Egyptian life by a respected scholar.

Peter Clayton and Martin Price. *The Seven Wonders of the Ancient World*. New York: Barnes and Noble, 1993. A general study of these famous monuments, with many insights into the Pyramids and the Alexandrian lighthouse.

Judith Crosher. *Technology in the Time of Ancient Egypt*. New York: Raintree, 1998. A general look at the building tools and labor-saving devices available to the ancient Egyptians.

Rosalie David. *Handbook to Life in Ancient Egypt*. New York: Facts On File, 2003. A very easy-to-read general survey of most aspects of Egyptian life, including arts, artisans, architecture, crafts, and more.

I.E.S. Edwards. *The Pyramids of Egypt*. New York: Penguin, 1993. A classic work about the Pyramids, by one of the leading Egyptologists of the twentieth century.

Zahi A. Hawass. *The Mysteries of Abu Simbel: Ramesses II and the Temples of the Rising Sun*. Cairo: American University in Cairo Press, 2001. The renowned Egyptian archaeologist delivers a synopsis of the temples and statues at one of the country's major ancient sites.

Geoffrey Killen. *Egyptian Woodworking and Furniture*. Princes Risborough, UK: Shire, 2008. A comprehensive, concise study of ancient Egyptian woodworkers and their craft.

Mark Lehner. *The Complete Pyramids*. London: Thames and Hudson, 2008. A highly illustrated and comprehensive source that covers all of the pyramids of Egypt, strengthened by data from Lehner's famous experiments re-creating ancient Egyptian construction techniques.

Lise Manniche. *Music and Musicians in Ancient Egypt*. London: Dover, 1992. Discusses the musical instruments in use in ancient Egypt and what is known about the social status and lives of the musicians themselves.

Anne Millard. *Mysteries of the Pyramids*. Brookfield, CT: Copper Beach Books, 1995. Aimed at basic readers, this book by a noted scholar is short but brightly illustrated and filled with interesting facts about the Pyramids and ancient Egyptian life.

Gay Robins. *The Art of Ancient Egypt*. Cambridge, MA: Harvard University Press, 2008. One of the leading experts on ancient Egyptian art delivers an informative and very readable book.

Jane Shuter. *Life in an Egyptian Workers' Village*. Chicago: Heinemann Library, 2005. Examines what life was like in the residential areas that were erected near the major construction sites in ancient Egypt.

Eugen Strouhal. *Life of the Ancient Egyptians*. Norman: University of Oklahoma Press, 1992. A general study of ancient Egyptian life that features several extended discussions of various craftsmen and artists.

Richard H. Wilkinson. *The Complete Temples of Ancient Egypt*. London: Thames and Hudson, 2000. A comprehensive source that discusses all kinds of ancient Egyptian temples.

Websites

Ancient Egyptian Architecture (www.greatbuildings.com/types/styles/egyptian.html). Provides links to separate pages, each of which describes an important ancient Egyptian structure. Included are the Great Pyramid of Khufu, Hatshepsut's Temple, the temples at Karnak, and several others.

Ancient Egyptian Jewelry Design (www.allaboutgemstones.com/jewelry_history_egyptian.html). Contains several photos of beautiful Egyptian jewelry pieces, plus some useful commentary on when and why they were made.

Ancient Egyptian Woodworking (www.skillspublish.com.au/Ancient%20Egyptian%20Woodworking.pdf). This excellent source discusses the tools used by Egyptian carpenters and how they were used.

Building in Ancient Egypt (www.reshafim.org.il/ad/egypt/building). Discusses the basic building materials and techniques used in ancient Egypt. Also provides links to a wide range of other topics relating to life and work in ancient Egypt.

The Colossi of Memnon (www.akhet.co.uk/memnon.htm). Contains some excellent photos of these huge statues and tells the story of the Greek myth associated with them.

The Discovery of the Tombs of the Pyramid Builders at Giza (www.guardians.net/hawass/buildtomb.htm). Renowned Egyptian archaeologist Zahi Hawass describes the recent discovery of a cemetery used by the workers who built the Giza pyramids.

Egyptian Painting (www.mnsu.edu/emuseum/prehistory/egypt/artisans/painting.htm). A useful general introduction to the subject, with references and links to other Internet sites.

Imhotep (www.touregypt.net/feature stories/imhotep.htm). An excellent, readable overview of the legendary Egyptian architect, vizier, and builder of the Step Pyramid.

The Pyramids: The Inside Story (www.pbs.org/wgbh/nova/pyramid). An informational and entertaining resource sponsored by the prestigious television science program *NOVA*, including information on Egyptologist Mark Lehner and his groundbreaking studies and experiments related to ancient Egyptian construction.

Index

Picture Credits

About the Author

Historian Don Nardo is best known for his books for young people about the ancient and medieval worlds. These include volumes on the arts of ancient cultures, including Mesopotamian arts and literature, Egyptian sculpture and monuments, Greek temples, Roman amphitheaters, medieval castles, and general histories of sculpture, painting, and architecture through the ages. Nardo lives with his wife, Christine, in Massachusetts.